GIFTS &
Heirlooms
in Cross-Stitch & Needlepoint

GIFTS & Heirlooms

in Cross-Stitch & Needlepoint

MARSHALL CAVENDISH

This edition published in 1995 by
Marshall Cavendish Books, London
(a division of Marshall Cavendish Partworks Ltd)

Copyright © Marshall Cavendish 1995
Foreword copyright © Melinda Coss 1995

ISBN 1 85435 833 2

British Library Cataloguing in Publication Data:
A catalogue record for this book is available from
the British Library

Printed and bound in Italy

Some of this material has previously appeared in
the Marshall Cavendish partwork *Discovering Needlecraft*

Contents

Foreword

Melinda Coss

In our highly technological age an 'embroidery epidemic' has to be considered a phenomenon. Yet here we are, nearly at the year 2000, and everywhere you look people are sitting with needles and threads, as cosy now, under electric light bulbs, as they were a hundred years ago, stitching below the glow of an oil lamp.

'What's the fascination?' ask the uninitiated. But how do you explain the pleasure of transforming richly coloured threads into finely patterned and textured fabrics? Stitching, as any embroiderer will tell you, is obsessive, and both cross-stitching and needlepoint, with their simple, repetitive techniques, provides a comforting and therapeutic way to end a stressful day. Add to that the portability of a needlework project, the low cost of the materials and the satisfaction of making a special gift at the same time as producing a personalised heirloom, and it is perhaps not so surprising that needlecraft remains one of our most popular leisure activities.

Through my years as a needlecraft designer I have established that most stitchers share two major problems. The first is that they always underestimate their own abilities and the second is that they never have enough designs to choose from. This book should provide the solutions.

Packed with bright ideas and delicious projects, the book has something that will appeal to all tastes and levels of skill. It talks you through the stitching process from beginning to end, and what is not explained in words is there for all to see on the clearly graphed charts and beautiful photographs. It is also interspersed with hints and tips that will help to ensure that your stitched designs have a highly professional finish.

Many stitchers dread the making-up process; but often we only have to succeed at something once to realise that we are cleverer than we think. This confidence can lead on to all manner of new and satisfying accomplishments. The secret is to read the instructions carefully and to begin with a relatively simple tent stitch project like a greetings card. Take it step-by-step and, before you know it, you will find yourself, like a true expert, making up cushions and framing pictures to give as presents to your friends and relations.

Needlecraft is not simply about following patterns and using specific materials. It is also a valuable means of self-expression. You can stitch with wools, ribbons, silks and even strips of fabric, and you don't have to use special embroidery materials to achieve pleasing results. Try using the geometric motifs and techniques in this book to create your own individual statement. If your passion is for cross-stitch, remember that needlepoint charts work equally well in cross-stitch so, if you prefer, you can stitch canvaswork designs on the nearest count of aida fabric, or vice versa. You could also incorporate beads into your cross-stitch or work the motifs on waste canvas on bed- or table-linen. Personalise designs by incorporating a special message in a gift sampler to commemorate an important event. Once you gain confidence, you will realise that your only limitation is your imagination.

On a final note, if you have children around the house, do share your skills with them. I, for one, hope to live long enough to see my grandchildren stitching, although I suspect they may be doing so on electro-magnetic fibres with automatic laser-powered needle pushers. In the meantime, enjoy yourselves and this book, which will provide you with many hours of inspiration and a wealth of ideas for gifts to give to loved ones and friends on anniversaries and other special occasions.

Melinda Coss.

The Projects

Introduction

Needlepoint and cross-stitch are two of the most popular of the multitude of embroidery techniques. Because they are straightforward to work, they are simple enough for the beginner, but their lasting appeal has much to do with the fact that both are extremely versatile, and their beauty is undeniable.

The projects that have been collected together here provide a wide variety of items to stitch, and they are designed to appeal to beginners and needlepoint addicts alike. The clear charts are easy to follow and the finished pieces can be enjoyed for years to come by a member of your family or a lucky friend. Hand-stitched items are popular presents and those in this book range from greetings cards that can be completed in an evening to a selection of beautiful, more intricate floral cushions and pictures.

Some of the projects would make welcome gifts for a newlywed couple, while others could be made and presented to special friends on an anniversary, always an occasion worth celebrating.

There are also presents suitable for a special baby or child. The Nursery Rhyme quilt would be a welcome addition to any child's room, while the Aesop's fables pictures will spark off bed-time stories galore. And both would most likely become treasured family heirlooms in years to come.

The more complicated projects have in them various elements that can be extracted and used individually to make small items such as greetings cards or miniature pictures. Some of the designs lend themselves to being stitched separately and then grouped: the plants from the garden flower cushion, for example, could be mounted individually and hung as pictures. If you are new to these techniques, you may want to study the various stitches detailed on pages 105–25 before you begin. Then choose your project, study the chart, pick up your needle and start to stitch. But be warned: needlepoint and cross-stitch can be addictive!

A NOTE ABOUT THREADS

The threads specified in each project have been used to work the items shown in the photographs. If you are unable to purchase the materials exactly as specified, it will still be possible to work the project, but the look may be somewhat altered. Most ranges of yarns and threads have similar or equivalent colours from which to choose, but the colour match may not be exact.

Wildflower cushion

Meadow and woodland flowers native to the English countryside make this cushion a perfect gift for a special gardening friend.

Wildflower cushion

Paterna Persian yarn – see Key, below right, for colours and numbers of skeins

YOU WILL NEED

- **50 × 50cm 10-gauge single canvas**
- **Paterna Persian yarn – see Key, below right, for colours and numbers of skeins**
- **Tapestry needle**
- **50 × 50cm medium-weight backing fabric**
- **45 × 45cm cushion pad**

Stitched entirely in continental tent stitch, this cushion is very satisfying to make and, although it appears to be complicated, the stylised wildflower design is easy enough for the least nimble-fingered stitcher to follow. This colourful cushion would make an ideal present for any-one who is interested in gardening or the natural world and will look equally at home in a formal sitting room setting and in a kitchen or conservatory.

STARTING POINTS

On the chart opposite, each coloured square represents a single stitch, worked across one intersection of canvas. Before starting to stitch, you may find it helpful to mount your canvas on a frame (see page 18). This will not only make working easier but will also help prevent the canvas from distorting.

Use three strands of yarn throughout and keep the back of your work free from knots. Work each stitch in two movements: pass the needle from the front of the work to the back and pull the yarn right through, before passing the needle back to the front again. Try to maintain an even tension as you stitch.

SIMPLE STITCHING

Start at the centre of the design and work out-wards to keep the design central to your canvas square and to avoid distorting the canvas. Stitch the central display of white primroses and rosehips (see How to start

It is a good idea to mount swatches of all the yarn colours you will be using on a project card (similar to the examples, right) and label each one with the skein number. You will find this use-ful to refer to as you stitch.

stitching, page 12), followed by the red and yellow edging. Once you have a particular colour in your needle, stitch other areas of the same colour, if they are nearby. Do not dot your stitches around the canvas too much, but move on to adjacent areas wherever possible.

When you have completed the central square, work your way clockwise or anti-clockwise round the surrounding border of meadow flowers. Choose an area as a starting point, such as the pale pink dog rose, and work your way round to meet it again. Once the flowers have been finished, stitch the red and yellow outer edging. Finally, when all the details of the design have been stitched, work the rich blue background. Hold your finished work up to the light to check if you have missed any stitches – add single stitches to fill any gaps.

KEY

Paterna Persian yarns: colours and skeins, one skein each except where indicated:

A	604 (2)	**I**	764	**S**	692 (2)
B	311	**K**	544	**T**	694 (2)
C	312	**L**	772	**U**	704
D	756	**M**	841	**V**	545
E	693 (2)	**N**	600	**W**	263 (2)
F	473	**O**	602 (2)	**X**	941
G	840 (4)	**P**	935	**Y**	221
H	934	**R**	726 (4)	**Z**	500 (19)

BACKING FABRICS

When you are choosing a backing fabric for your cushion, the first thing to consider is the weight of the fabric. Make sure the fabric is strong enough to be sewn to stitched canvas, as otherwise the seams of your cushion may split. A medium-weight material is best, such as a good furnishing or curtain fabric, which will withstand everyday wear and tear. The second factor that should influence your choice is colour. Choose a colour that complements the stitched canvas, yet will not detract from the design. Remember that darker colours look rich and splendid in any setting and will not get dirty too quickly.

To add an individual touch to your cushion, you could stitch a length of piping round the seam, or sew some tassels on to the corners. Ready-made extras like these are available from department stores.

Follow the graph chart above, using the colours as indicated to produce this attractive wildflower design. One coloured square on the chart represents a single continental tent stitch. Start at the centre of the chart and work outwards.

HOW TO START STITCHING

1 To find the centre of your canvas square, fold it in half and then in half again. The centre point of your canvas corresponds with the centre point of the design chart.

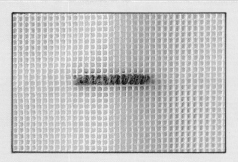

2 Start at the centre of the design, from the stems of the four white wild pansies, and work your way outwards. Start by stitching the medium green of the stems (E:693).

3 Then branch outwards in the same colour to start the leaves. Begin by working two single stitches, two squares apart, above the line and two single stitches below.

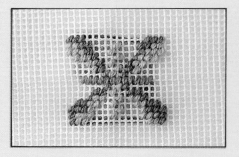

4 Moving to the next adjacent colour areas, work the lighter green of the stems (T:694). Then complete each leaf in turn, filling in the shaded areas using darker green (O:602).

5 Stitch the dark yellow centres of the flowers (R:726), then fill the bright yellow areas (L:772). Work in a clockwise circle, moving to the ivory petals (D:756).

6 When you have stitched all the details of the design, fill in the background areas in dark blue (Z:500). Try to stitch in blocks of colour if you can for a neater finish.

HOW TO MAKE UP THE CUSHION

1 Place backing fabric and canvas right sides together, match up edges and tack together. Sew round three sides in backstitch close to the edge of the stitched design. This may be done on a sewing machine. Remove tacking stitches and trim seams and corners.

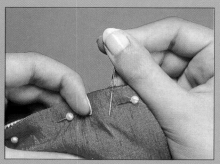

2 Turn cushion through to the right side and gently push out corners using a blunt point. Insert cushion pad through the opening. Finally turn seams in and oversew the open edge in small, neat stitches using matching sewing thread.

BLOCKING

When you have finished all the stitching, remove your work from the frame. If it has become distorted despite being stretched on a frame, then it will need to be blocked.

To do this, you will first of all need to dampen the work by spraying it all over on the back with clean cold water. Then pin it face down on to a piece of soft board, using rust-proof tacks. Stretch the work gently and tack, starting at the top centre edge. Next pin the centre of the opposite edge, and finally the side edges. Working toward the corners, place tacks at 2.5cm intervals, pulling the canvas into shape. Check the shape of the canvas carefully as you go, making sure that it is square. Dampen the work once again, then leave it to dry thoroughly. Check that the canvas is completely dry before you remove the tacks, otherwise the canvas will distort again (see also pages 115–16).

Garden flower cushion

Colourful flowers and butterflies worked in half cross-stitch
create realistic details on this beautiful needlepoint cushion.

Garden flower cushion

YOU WILL NEED

- **42 × 42cm 12-gauge single canvas**
- **Paterna Persian yarn, one skein each of:**

Mauve D117	D137 Mid mauve
Pale mauve D147	903 Dark pink
Pale pink 955	905 Sugar pink
Pale yellow 714	712 Mid yellow
Dark yellow 710	950 Dark strawberry
Mid strawberry 952	221 Charcoal
Mid forest green 602	604 Pale forest green
Dark green 610	620 Emerald green
Dark brown 410	473 Fawn
Wood rose 922	920 Dark wood rose
White 260	

- **Two skeins each of:**

Deep blue 560	563 Light blue
Pine green 662	621 Shamrock green
Pale spice 855	

- **Three skeins each of:**

  Mid gold 734
- **Four skeins each of:**

  Pale gold 735
- **Tapestry needle**
- **40 × 40cm backing fabric**
- **33cm square cushion pad**

The fine detail in this delightful floral cushion gives it an almost painted look. The flowers depicted – petunias, campanulas and two forms of dianthus – have distinctive petal and leaf shapes, and will be familiar to all gardening enthusiasts. The butterflies are also stitched to look as realistic as possible – the one in the centre is a Red Admiral, the yellow ones at top and bottom are Brimstones, and the darker ones on each side are Purple Hairstreaks. The border is made up of stylised forget-me-nots on a trellis background.

The cushion, which measures 32cm square, is worked entirely in half cross-stitch with backstitch details for the butterflies' antennae. The design would look beautiful in any number of settings. It would suit cane or metalwork conservatory furniture as well as traditional or country-style furnishings in a living room. It would also look charming in a bedroom, perhaps on a small antique chair or on a bed covered with a plain bedspread.

PREPARING THE CANVAS

Before you begin stitching, bind the raw edges of the canvas with masking tape to prevent the wool yarn from catching on them as you work. If the yarn keeps snagging, it will gradually wear thin and will then not cover the canvas properly. Mount the canvas in a slate frame if you wish (see page 18). This has the advantage of stretching the canvas taut as you are stitching and will help to keep it in shape. It also means that you can speed up your stitching with one hand above and one below the canvas.

The colour chart for the centre panel of the garden flower design is shown on the opposite page; while the chart for the forget-me-not border is on the page following. Each square on the chart represents one half cross-stitch and the colours of Persian yarn to use are shown in the keys. To help you to follow the chart for the centre panel more easily, mark the horizontal and vertical centre lines on the canvas with tacking stitches and mark the corresponding centre of the chart with pencil. As a large number of shades of yarn has been used in this design, you may find it is useful to keep them on a project card. These are available from the haberdashery section of department stores or from needlecraft shops; alternatively,

White campanula is worked in the bottom right-hand corner of the cushion's centre panel. The glossy green leaves are a perfect contrast to the white and pale yellow flowers.

you can make your own by punching holes along a piece of card and looping yarn lengths of about 45cm through them. Label each colour with its shade number and name, and you will then find it more easily when you come to it on the chart. Some of the areas on the chart are worked using one strand each of two colours, and if you wish, these could also be added to the project organiser.

STITCHING THE CENTRE PANEL

To start off an area of stitching neatly, leave a short length of thread at the back of the canvas and work the first few stitches over it to hold it in place. To finish off, pass the needle through the last few stitches worked at the back and then cut the thread end off short. If you leave trailing threads at the back of the work, they will get caught up in subsequent stitching and may be pulled through to the front of the canvas or cause a lumpy finish.

Try to finish off one area of colour before beginning the next. However, where there are lots of small areas of colour, as in the flowers and the butterflies, you may find it easier to thread up several needles with different

KEY

Paterna Persian yarn, as used in the centre panel of the Garden flower cushion:

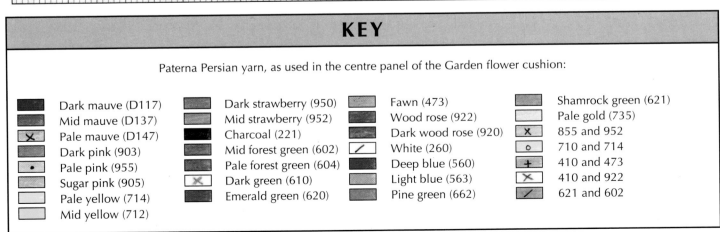

Dark mauve (D117)	Dark strawberry (950)	Fawn (473)	Shamrock green (621)
Mid mauve (D137)	Mid strawberry (952)	Wood rose (922)	Pale gold (735)
Pale mauve (D147)	Charcoal (221)	Dark wood rose (920)	855 and 952
Dark pink (903)	Mid forest green (602)	White (260)	710 and 714
Pale pink (955)	Pale forest green (604)	Deep blue (560)	410 and 473
Sugar pink (905)	Dark green (610)	Light blue (563)	410 and 922
Pale yellow (714)	Emerald green (620)	Pine green (662)	621 and 602
Mid yellow (712)			

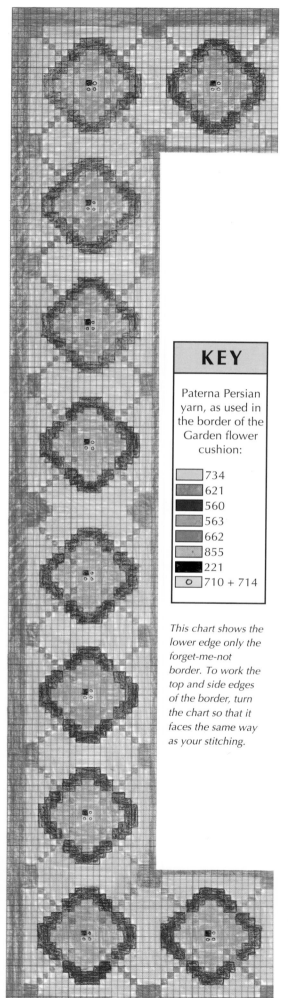

*This chart shows the
lower edge only the
forget-me-not
border. To work the
top and side edges
of the border, turn
the chart so that it
faces the same way
as your stitching.*

colours and use each colour as you come to it
on the chart. Keep the needles you are not
using pinned in the canvas margin, well away
from the stitching area.

Using two strands of Persian yarn in your
needle throughout, begin stitching the Red
Admiral butterfly at the centre of the design.
Part of the shading in its wings is worked by
blending two different colours in the needle:
use one strand of wood rose (922) and one
strand of dark brown (410) for this.

When the Red Admiral is complete, count
the canvas threads carefully to begin the pink
dianthus in the top right-hand corner. The
leaves are worked in three shades of green
and the petals in three shades of pink. The
flower centres are a shade of yellow made by
combining one strand each of dark yellow
(710) and pale yellow (714) in the needle.
Work a Brimstone butterfly on the left of the
pink dianthus, combining dark brown and
fawn (473) for the body. Below the pink
dianthus, work a Purple Hairstreak butterfly.
As before, combine dark brown with fawn for
part of the body and wood rose with dark
brown for part of the wings.

Now stitch the white campanula in the bottom right-hand corner, combining dark yellow
and pale yellow for the flower centres. The
variegated leaves are worked in four shades
of green. Stitch another Brimstone butterfly to
the left of this flower and then the red
dianthus in the bottom left-hand corner. The
spiky leaves are in three shades of green, and
the flower centres are made up of two shades
of yellow as before, as well as charcoal.

To complete the centre design, stitch
another Purple Hairstreak butterfly as before
and then work the final floral motif – the
petunia. Shades of mauve are used for the
petals, with blended yellows for the centres.
The leaves are three shades of the darker
greens. Finally add single stitches in charcoal
for the tips of the butterflies' antennae. You
can now fill in the background around the
flowers and butterflies in pale gold (735). Use
one strand of charcoal and backstitch to work
the butterflies' antennae.

THE FORGET-ME-NOT BORDER

The inner band of the border is worked as a
single row of half cross-stitch in shamrock
green (621). Add the inner part of the trellis in
the same colour. The forget-me-nots around
the border are stitched in deep blue (560) and
light blue (563) with pale spice (855) around

*A large Red Admiral butterfly is worked in the
centre of the cushion. The wings are tipped with
dark and mid strawberry red and dotted with
charcoal and white stitches.*

the centres. The centres are worked with two
shades of yellow as for the other flowers, but
the fourth stitch in each centre is charcoal,
which should be worked when all the other
stitching is complete. Complete the outer part
of the trellis and the outer border in pine
green (662), and then fill in the background
with the mid gold yarn (734).

MAKING UP THE CUSHION

Block the canvas if necessary to restore it to its
original shape (see pages 115–6). Trim the
excess canvas from around the design to leave
a 1.5cm seam allowance and cut the backing
fabric to match. With right sides facing, pin
and backstitch the backing fabric to the
canvas, leaving an opening at the bottom
edge for turning through. Clip across the top
corners to remove the excess fabric and turn
the cushion cover through to the right side.
Insert the cushion pad through the opening in
the bottom edge and slip stitch the opening to
close it. If you wish, you can sew a twisted
cord around the edges to cover the seam. If
so, you will need to buy 1.4m of cord.

Squirrel cushion

*The rich colours and stylised border of this plump cushion will add
a touch of medieval splendour to a formal living room.*

YOU WILL NEED

- 45 × 45cm 10-gauge single canvas
- Paterna Persian yarn in the following colours: one skein each of: 430, 552, 722 and 880
- Two skeins each of: D522, 661, 723 and 883
- Three skeins each of: 263 and 704
- Five skeins each of: 571 and 772
- Eight skeins of: 901
- Tapestry needle
- 45 × 45cm backing fabric
- 40cm square cushion pad

Squirrel cushion

This beautiful cushion was inspired by the designs of many medieval tapestries, which traditionally included small animals and intricate floral patterns stitched against a plain background. The colours too – rich burgundy and blues, studded with details worked in delicate shades of yellow, green and cream – follow those of wall hangings stitched centuries ago.

The cushion is worked in half cross-stitch on 10-gauge single canvas. Find the centre of your canvas square by folding the canvas in half lengthways and then in half again widthways. Mark the centre with two lines of running stitch which cross each other at the centre. Then stretch the canvas on a frame, if you wish (see below). By working with the canvas on a frame and stitching from the centre of the canvas outwards, you can avoid distorting the canvas too much.

HALF CROSS-STITCH

Start by threading your needle using all three strands of brown yarn (722). Work with a length of yarn no longer than 50cm because if the thread is any longer, it could knot or wear thin. Starting at the centre of the canvas where the two lines of running stitch cross, begin with the squirrel, which is stitched in several shades of brown. Use three strands of yarn throughout. Secure the end of your first thread by working a few stitches over it at the back. Follow the chart opposite, using the key as a guide to match the colours with their thread numbers. One coloured square on the chart represents a single half cross-stitch. Work one stitch over one intersection of the canvas. Continue to work half cross-stitch in horizontal rows across the body of the squirrel.

Half cross-stitch is literally that – the first half of a cross-stitch. A horizontal row is worked like the first half of a row of ordinary cross-stitch (see page 105). This will give a row of vertical stitches on the back of your canvas. Similarly, a row of half cross-stitch

HOW TO MOUNT CANVAS IN A SLATE FRAME

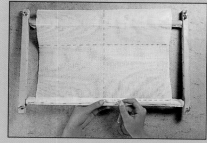

1 *Having marked the centre of your canvas, place one edge over the tape on one rod and sew canvas and tape together with running stitch or backstitch.*

2 *Sew canvas to tape on the opposite rod in the same way. Then roll the rods until the canvas is centred and taut. Fix the rods in position by tightening the wing nuts.*

To work the central square, follow the chart on the right. The key will help you to identify colours. The chart on the left is for the bottom left-hand corner of the red border. For the other three corners, turn this chart round and repeat the design.

KEY

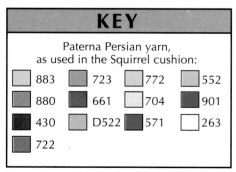

Paterna Persian yarn,
as used in the Squirrel cushion:

▢	883	▣	723	▢	772	▣	552
▣	880	■	661	▢	704	■	901
■	430	▣	D522	■	571	▢	263
▣	722						

worked vertically down the canvas produces a row of horizontal stitches on the back.

Complete each solid block of colour before moving on to the next one, carefully following the colour chart above. After you have finished one patch of colour, if there are no more areas of that shade nearby, finish off the thread neatly on the back. Start a new thread by passing the needle under a few previously worked stitches on the back.

When the squirrel is complete, move on to work the white, yellow and blue flowers surrounding the squirrel. Then fill in the leaves in the two shades of green. When you have finished all the details of the central square design, work the background in navy blue, stitching in rows for an even tension. You should aim to complete each corner of the inner square immediately surrounding the squirrel before moving on to the next one. Only move on to the outer border once you have completed the inner square.

Stitch the details of the border first, following the chart on page 18. The chart for the bottom left-hand corner has been illustrated but since this is a repeating border, it is easy to work the other corners using the same chart. Stitch the bottom left-hand corner of the border first. Turn the chart round to work the other corners. When the details of the border are complete, fill in the dark burgundy background. Finally, stitch the narrow outer border in navy, yellow and cream.

When you have stitched the whole design, you are ready to block the canvas (stretch it into shape). It is rare for finished work not to need some reshaping. This involves dampening the canvas and pinning it to a board, shaping it into a perfect square to dry. For tips on how to block a canvas successfully, follow the steps on the right and see pages 115–16.

MAKING UP THE CUSHION

The final stage is to make the stitched canvas up into a cushion (see also page 12). Place the canvas and backing fabric right sides together and pin in place. Tack the two pieces together along the line where the stitched canvas ends. Stitch around three sides, either with backstitch or on a sewing machine. Trim the seam allowance to 1cm and clip across the corners to reduce bulk. Insert the cushion pad, pushing it right into the corners of the cover. Turn in the edges of the unstitched side and pin together so no raw edges are visible. Slip stitch the two folds together, using a matching sewing thread. Fasten off the stitching firmly with a couple of backstitches to make the seam secure and your cushion is ready to be presented to a special friend – if you can bear to give it away!

BLOCKING A CANVAS

1 Dampen the stitched canvas lightly (by rolling it in a damp towel or spraying it with warm water), then stretch it into shape as much as possible by hand, gripping the edges firmly and pulling the canvas along opposite edges and corners.

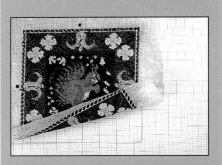

2 Using a pencil, mark up a piece of graph paper, pinned on a 5-ply wooden board or similar, with a square the size of the cushion. Mark centre of square and centre of each side. Place the canvas on the paper and pin in position along edges of square.

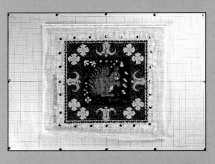

3 Stretch the canvas until the edges follow those of the square and pin it in place with drawing pins. Use a set square (or the edge of a magazine) to check that the corners form angles of 90 degrees. Let the canvas dry before unpinning it.

HELPFUL

Every needleworker will appreciate the benefits of using a frame for keeping needlework or embroidery at a constant tension. Large floor frames, such as that shown right, will adjust to the stitcher's chair height and can be tilted for easy access to both the front and back of the work. Rectangular or circular hand frames may be used by themselves or clamped in a floor stand, as right. All frames have knobs or wing nuts on the joints so you can loosen them to let canvas or fabric in, then tighten them again.

HINTS

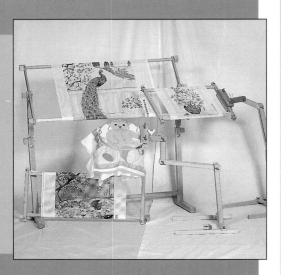

Baroque cushion

*Full of rich colour and intricate patterning, this superb 'baroque' cushion
would make a sumptuous present for a special birthday.*

Baroque cushion

Beginners and experienced stitchers alike will find much to enjoy in making this beautiful cushion. It is worked entirely in half cross-stitch, so is not at all difficult to stitch, but the interest lies in the glorious combination of colours in the fruit design which will appeal to all those who enjoy intricate patterns. The ornate design with its dark background and richly coloured fruit and leaves has a definite baroque feel to it, especially with the addition of lots of gold curlicues. The gold twisted cord which edges the cushion adds a further elaborate touch. The finished cushion measures 38cm square, and would look best in a traditional setting with furnishings in deep colours.

PREPARING THE CANVAS

Before you begin stitching, bind the raw edges of the canvas with masking tape or bias binding so that the yarn does not snag on them; if it keeps catching on the rough edges, the yarn will wear thin and will not then cover the canvas properly. Mount the canvas in a slate frame if you wish (see page 18). This will keep it taut while you are stitching, give it a neater finish and prevent it from becoming distorted. It will also help to speed up your stitching as you can then have one hand below and one above the canvas.

The fruit design is shown on the chart opposite. Each coloured square equals one half cross-stitch and the key below indicates which shade of Persian yarn to use for each part of the design. Mark the centre of the canvas horizontally and vertically with lines of running stitch, and mark the chart in the same way in pencil to help you to position your

YOU WILL NEED

- **48 × 48cm 10-gauge single canvas**
- **Paterna Persian yarn, one skein each of:**

Pale beige 465	735 Very pale gold
Pale olive 643	D546 Dull green
Dark green 660	950 Bright red
Dusty pink 912	741 Old gold
Very pale yellow 763	692 Loden green
Very pale pink 326	762 Lemon yellow
Dull gold 751	844 Coral
Lilac 322	630 Spring green

- **Two skeins each of:**

Dark yellow 700	726 Mid yellow
Old rose D234	471 Toast brown

- **Three skeins each of:**

Burgundy 900	Black 220

- **Tapestry needle**
- **41 × 41cm backing fabric**
- **38cm square cushion pad**
- **1.6m gold twisted cord**

KEY

Paterna Persian yarn, as used in the Baroque cushion:

o	Pale beige – 465 (A)		·	Very pale yellow – 763 (L)
x	Very pale gold – 735 (B)			Burgundy – 900 (M)
	Pale olive green – 643 (C)			Toast brown – 471 (N)
/	Dull green – D546 (D)			Old rose – D234 (O)
	Dark green – 660 (E)			Loden green – 692 (P)
	Spring green – 630 (F)		S	Very pale pink – 326 (Q)
	Bright red – 950 (G)		▼	Lemon yellow – 762 (R)
o	Dusty pink – 912 (H)		T	Dull gold – 751 (S)
I	Dark yellow – 700 (I)		+	Coral – 844 (T)
^	Old gold – 741 (J)			Lilac – 322 (U)
	Mid yellow – 726 (K)			Black – 220 (V)

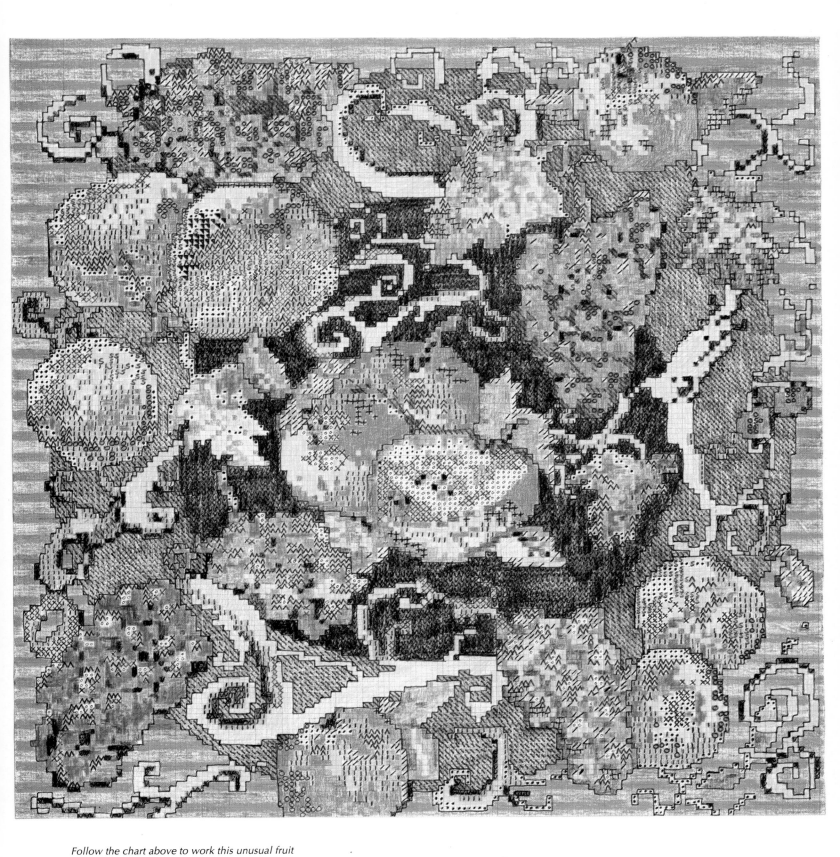

Follow the chart above to work this unusual fruit design. The key on the opposite page shows the shades of Paterna Persian yarn to use for each coloured square on the chart.

STITCH DETAILS

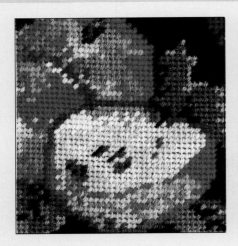

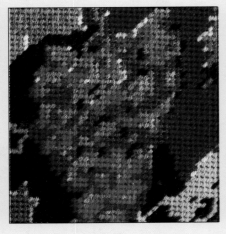

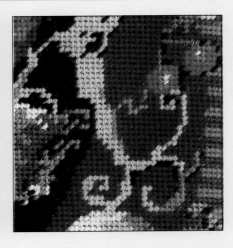

Two whole apples and one cut apple are worked in the centre of the cushion cover. These are stitched in bright red, with highlights in various shades of gold and yellow.

The bunch of grapes in the top right-hand corner of the cushion cover is worked in burgundy, lilac and dusty pink with dull green and old gold speckles.

Mid yellow and dark yellow are used to work the curlicues that link the fruit motifs. These are set off by the black and burgundy backgrounds and the old rose and toast brown stripes

colours correctly when you begin following the chart. Use a bright-coloured sewing thread when you work the running stitch lines, which can be worked over and then removed when the design is complete.

As so many different shades of yarn are used to work this cushion cover, you will find it helpful to sort them on to project cards. You can either buy these ready-made or make your own by punching holes along the edges of long pieces of card. Cut the yarn into 45cm lengths and loop them through the holes, then mark the shade names and numbers next to them. In this way, you will be able to find each colour easily as you come to it on the chart.

STITCHING THE FRUIT DESIGN

Begin stitching at the centre of the chart with the shaded red apple, using two strands of yarn in the needle. Work one area at a time, and take care not to pass long strands of yarn from one part of the design to the other as this will make the work too bulky. As there are a lot of small blocks of colour used in this design, you will find it quicker to stitch if you thread several adjoining colours up at the same time, and use each one as you need it. Needles that are not being used can be secured in the margin of the canvas, well away from the area you are working on, so that the threads do not get caught up in sub-

sequent stitching and cause an unsightly effect on the right side of the work.

When you have finished stitching the first apple, work the one behind it and then the cut apple in front, adding the leaves around the edge. Follow the chart carefully, counting the squares of each colour. Next work the golden curlicues at the top of the apples, moving on to the peaches at the top left and the purple-coloured grapes at the top right. You can either stitch the black background as you progress or fill it in when you have finished all the fruit. Move down to the paler-coloured grapes and the curlicues below the central apples, filling in the black background around them.

Continue working the peaches, grapes, apples and curlicues towards the outer edges of the design, filling in the background in burgundy (900). There are also two cherries on the far right-hand side which should be worked now. Complete the cushion cover by stitching the striped background in old rose (D234) and toast brown (471).

MAKING UP THE CUSHION COVER

Remove the completed needlepoint from the frame if you used one. If your work needs stretching, block it as described on page 115. If the work has not become too distorted, it may just need pressing carefully from the wrong side to restore it to its original square.

Trim the excess canvas from around the stitched design, leaving a 1.5cm seam allowance all round. Trim the backing fabric to the same size. With right sides facing, pin the backing fabric to the needlepoint and stitch together around three sides with backstitch. Clip the corners to remove the excess fabric and turn the cushion cover through to the right side. Insert the cushion pad and sew up the fourth side with slip stitch, leaving a short gap for tucking in the ends of the twisted cord. Sew on the twisted cord with slip stitch, hiding the raw ends in the gap (see page 12).

be creative

To accentuate the luxurious baroque feel of this cushion, you could add some thick golden tassels to each corner, choosing them to match the gold twisted cord.

For an alternative appearance, it is quite straightforward to make your own tassels from yarn (see page 119).

Choose a selection of colours from the yarns used for the cushion cover so that they tone in beautifully. For example, you could use burgundy (900), lilac (322) and bright red (950), or dark yellow (700), old gold (741) and mid yellow (726).

Victorian sampler

Step back in time and create a period sampler
with traditional motifs, borders and lettering.

Victorian sampler

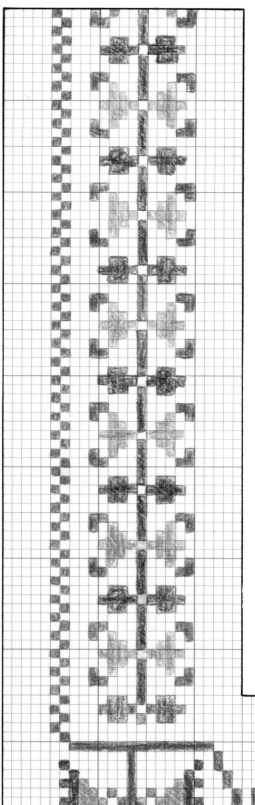

*T*his magnificent cross-stitch sampler is based on traditional Victorian motifs and borders, combined with two different styles of alphabet and a set of numerals. Stylised birds – doves, peacocks, bluebirds, a swan and a cockerel – are featured, each with its own distinctive characteristics. The trees include both conifers and tree-of-life designs, while the various borders are either simple and geometric or more floral. A flower basket and an ornate urn are also incorporated into the sampler along with tulip and carnation motifs and single geometric devices.

An alphabet of capital letters is stitched in blue, while another, of lower-case letters, together with a set of numerals, is worked in a soft pink. As well as looking decorative, these letters may well be useful in other cross-stitch or needlepoint projects where you want to add initials, words or dates.

To enhance the Victorian feel of this sampler, lovely soft colours have been chosen for the embroidery – sage greens, rose pinks, old golds and mid blues. The evenweave fabric is a natural-coloured aida which gives the impression of an antique linen fabric. A simple dark wooden frame without a mount works best with this kind of sampler, as it does not detract from the detail in the embroidery and is also in keeping with the way traditional samplers were originally displayed.

BEFORE YOU BEGIN

Oversew or bind the edges of the aida fabric to prevent them from fraying as you stitch.

YOU WILL NEED

- **44 × 50cm 14-count natural-coloured aida fabric**
- **Madeira 6-stranded embroidery cotton, one skein each of:**

Mustard 2203	2213 Dark mustard
Pinky brown 2312	0407 Crimson
Rose pink 0812	1712 Dull blue
Mid blue 1012	1203 Jade
Pale sage green 1604	

- **Two skeins of:**

  Dark sage green 1602
- **Tapestry needle**
- **Slate frame**

Fold the fabric in half each way and mark the centre horizontal and vertical lines with running stitches in a bright-coloured sewing thread. This will help you when you are counting the stitches from the chart, and can be easily removed when the sampler is complete. Mark the centre lines on the chart in pencil to correspond. Stretch the fabric in a slate frame so that it is kept taut as you stitch.

The border below runs along the lower edge of the sampler. It features stylised carnations worked in crimson, rose pink and dark sage green. The side border is stitched in mustard, dark mustard and pale sage green.

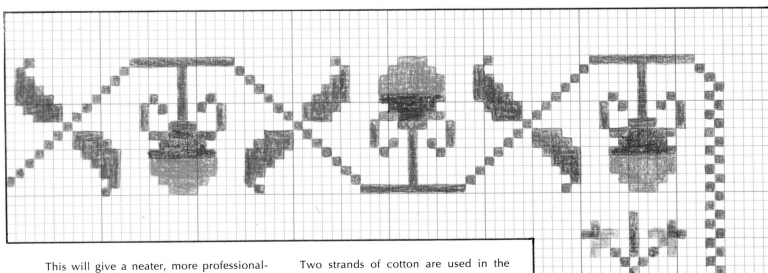

This will give a neater, more professional-looking finish, and will enable you to see the whole design as you progress (see page 18).

The sampler is shown as a chart on pages 88–9. Each symbol on the chart equals one cross-stitch, which is worked over one square of the aida fabric. Count the squares with symbols and the spaces in between them very carefully, as accuracy is important if all the borders are to join up correctly. The spacing between the letters and numerals is important, too, to give a balanced look to the alphabets.

STITCHING THE SAMPLER

It is a good idea to work the sampler from the centre outwards, as you can then be sure that it will be correctly positioned on the fabric. The crimson (0407) heart is a suitable motif to begin with; as it is slightly below the centre marked point on the chart, count out the number of aida squares from the centre down to the top of the heart and start stitching here.

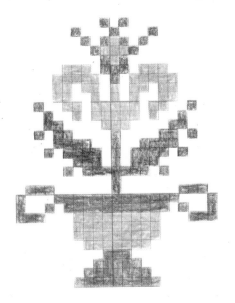

Two strands of cotton are used in the needle for the cross-stitching. To begin your work neatly, leave a short end of the embroidery cotton at the back of the fabric and make the first few stitches over it to secure it. To finish off, pass the needle under the last few stitches at the back of the work. Stitch one area of colour at a time, and do not take long lengths of thread across the back between areas. These will get caught up in subsequent stitching and may show through at the front when the sampler is complete.

When the heart is complete, add the ribbons in rose pink (0812) and the doves in mid blue (1012) and pinky brown (2312). Counting outwards from the doves, work the cockerel on the left and the swan on the right. Complete the row with the bluebirds in mid blue. Next work the wavy line above the birds in pale sage green (1604), and work the lower-case alphabet and the numerals in rose pink. Count the spaces between the letters very carefully and add the small geometric motifs in dark mustard (2213) and dull blue (1712) when you come to them on the chart.

The twisted border between the two alphabets is worked in dark sage green (1602) and pale sage green, and the capital letters are mid blue. Add a geometric motif, a tulip and a flower basket at the end of the alphabet, as well as three tiny diamond shapes in pinky brown. To complete the top of the sampler, stitch the strawberry border in rose pink, crimson and dark sage green.

The upper border of the sampler shows a row of strawberry motifs. The border for the right-hand side is worked with a different pattern from the left-hand side, but is stitched in the same colours. The flower in the urn on the final row of the sampler is worked in crimson and rose pink.

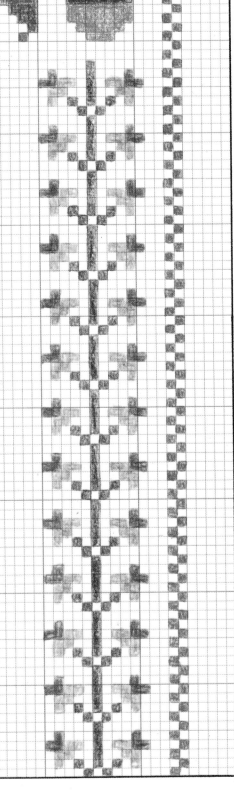

27

You can now continue with the lower half of the sampler. The border below the row of birds is worked in dark sage green. Then comes a row of trees in different colours and patterns. The central tree is worked entirely in dark sage green, while the ones on either side are stitched in two colours. Smaller trees worked in pinky brown are placed between the five large ones. When the trees are complete, work a wavy geometric line of stitching, this time in the pale sage green, below them.

The final row of motifs in the sampler shows a flower urn in the centre and two splendid peacocks on either side. Work the peacocks in mid blue with dull blue for the tail and crest. The tail decorations are jade (1203) and dark mustard, the eyes are jade and the legs dark mustard. Two identical flowers in mustard (2203), dark sage green and jade come at the ends of this row. The lower border consists of carnation flowers in rose pink and crimson with dark sage green stems. To finish off the sampler, stitch the side borders. The inner borders are two different floral designs in shades of mustard and pale sage green, and the outer border is simply made up of alternating crosses worked in the dark sage green.

MAKING UP THE SAMPLER

Before you remove the sampler from the slate frame, check that you have not missed any of the cross-stitches, as these will be difficult to add once the fabric is mounted over card and the design is framed. Finish off all your thread ends neatly, weaving them into a few stitches

be creative

As well as showing skill in stitching, a sampler was also useful as a pattern library of motifs which could be used in other pieces of work.

You could extract any of the motifs on this sampler and stitch them on a small piece of evenweave or aida fabric to give as a greetings card, a bookmark or a pot pourri sachet. Use up the stranded cotton left over from this project, or odds and ends from your work basket.

The bookmark shown here was made by taking one carnation motif and a section of the right-hand border and working them on to a piece of white aida fabric. To balance the design you will need to add the alternating cross-stitches to the left-hand side of the border.

at the back of the work and cutting them off short so that they do not show through at the front and spoil the finished effect.

Take the fabric off the frame and press from the wrong side over a lightly padded surface so as not to flatten the stitches. Lace the sampler over a piece of acid-free mounting board (see page 125) and frame as you wish.

Conifer trees as well as tree-of-life motifs are worked in shades of sage green, mustard, pinky brown and jade in the band below.

Birthday card

*Surprise a friend with this cross-stitch
birthday card – it is a gift in itself!*

Birthday card

Everyone likes to receive birthday cards, and this hand-stitched design will brighten up any special day. The wrapped present is worked in counted cross-stitch using two strands of cotton in the needle, with the exception of the individual green crosses for the shadow, which are worked using a single strand.

BEFORE YOU START

Before you begin, mark the centre of your fabric by folding it into quarters, then work from the centre.

Leave a long end of thread on the wrong side and work over it with the first few stitches. Finish by threading the needle back through the last few stitches.

STITCHING THE DESIGN

You will probably find it easier to stitch the sides of the present first, followed by the ribbon on top and the yellow design on the wrapping paper and then fill in the inner blue areas. The green stitches create a shadow at the base of the parcel. The single crosses along the outer edges of the 'shadow' are worked using a single strand of cotton.

MAKING UP THE CARD

Press the fabric lightly over a padded surface such as a folded terry towel. Trim excess fabric from around the design so that it fits

inside the card with the design in the centre of the aperture. Leave at least two blank squares of white aida all the way round the edges. Sparingly spread fabric glue over the central section of the card just inside the aperture and position it over the stitched work. Glue the edges of the back of the front flap and fold it over the fabric (see page 32).

You could insert a piece of blank paper on which to write a message by cutting a piece of paper slightly less than twice the size of one fold of the card and gluing it inside when you stick down the front flap. You could make a Christmas card by substituting red and green for the parcel and gold thread for the stars.

YOU WILL NEED

- **7.5 × 10cm 14-count white aida fabric**
- **Madeira 6-stranded embroidery cotton, one skein each of:**
  Pale red 0406   0513 Dark red
  Turquoise 1108   0905 Blue
  Dark blue 0904   0105 Yellow
  Green 1610
- **Tapestry needle**
- **Pre-cut card**
- **Fabric glue**

bright ideas

The jolly colours on the card are suitable for all ages, but if you are working it for a special birthday, you could position numbers around the top of the card to give it a more personal touch. Work the numbers to replace the stars on the chart using backstitch or cross-stitch and bright-coloured threads (see page 46 or page 88 for charted numbers).

Greetings card

*To send fond greetings to a special friend on a birthday or anniversary,
what could be more special – or personal – than a hand-crafted card?*

Greetings card

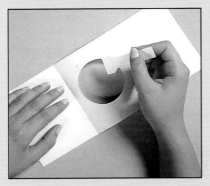

1 *Spread fabric glue sparingly over the central section of the card on the inside. Take care that no glue gets on to the face of the card.*

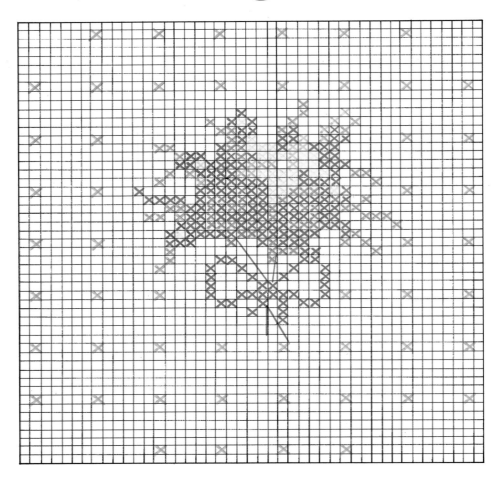

2 *Lay the finished embroidery right side up on a flat surface and position the glued area of the card on it so that the stitched design fits the aperture.*

S end a personal message to a close friend or relative with this pretty card: the cross-stitch flower bouquet design makes it suitable for almost any occasion.

The design is simple to stitch; just follow the chart and key above. One coloured square represents one stitch. Separate the strands of embroidery cotton and use two strands in your needle. Your card will be a joy to send and a pleasure to receive.

ORDER OF WORK

Start in the centre of the design, stitching the flower bouquet. Once you have finished this section, stitch the green crosses that form the background pattern. Finally, work the flower stems with a few straight stitches.

Follow the steps on the right to complete the card. Then, if you are feeling really creative, you could add an extra dimension to your handiwork by decorating the outside of the card mount.

Using felt pens, paints or coloured pencils, why not add a little border, following the embossed line around the circular aperture, or embellish one of the bottom corners of the card with a few tiny flowers?

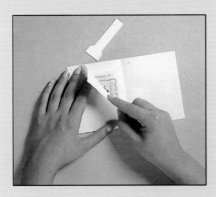

3 *On the inside, spread glue sparingly around edges of centre section, avoiding the area where the fabric shows through the aperture. Fold left-hand section of card over to cover fabric. Press down firmly to seal.*

YOU WILL NEED

- **7.5 × 10cm 18-count white aida fabric**
- **Madeira 6-stranded embroidery cotton, one skein each of:**
      Red 0309   0223 Dusty pink
  Light green 0699   0792 Blue
      Tan 0783   0744 Yellow
- **Tapestry needle**
- **Pre-cut card**
- **Fabric glue**

Pot pourri sachet

Quick and easy to sew, this simple cross-stitch sachet makes a delightful, sweetly scented gift for a special friend – and is far too pretty to hide away in a drawer!

YOU WILL NEED

- **11.5 × 23cm 14-count ivory aida fabric**
- **Madeira 6-stranded embroidery cotton, one skein each of:**

  Light blue 0800   0333 Violet
  Light green 0368   0600 Dark pink
  Pale pink 0604   0444 Yellow
  Orange 0740   0986 Dark green

- **Tapestry needle**
- **75cm cream lace, 2.5cm wide**
- **25g pot pourri or dried lavender**
- **White sewing thread**
- **Sharps needle**

Pot pourri sachet

A SINGLE CROSS-STITCH

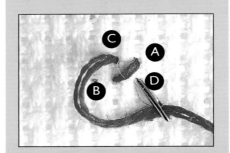

Make a diagonal stitch by bringing the needle out at A, inserting it at B, bringing the needle out at C and inserting it at D, crossing the first diagonal stitch. Work all the top diagonals in the same direction.

CROSS-STITCH IN ROWS

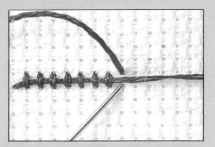

1 *(Back of work) Stitch a row of diagonal stitches, working from left to right. Leave a short length of thread when you make your first stitch and work the first few stitches over the loose end.*

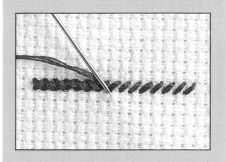

2 *Stitch a second row of diagonal stitches over the first row, working from right to left, to produce small, neat crosses with the top diagonals all in the same direction. Secure thread ends by passing the needle under several previously worked stitches.*

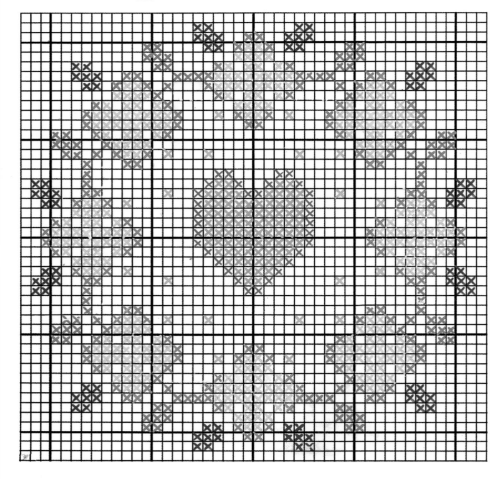

MAKING UP THE SACHET

Pin, then tack the lace in place round the edge of the unstitched piece of fabric, then put the stitched fabric face down on top. Stitch round three sides in backstitch. Turn the sachet right side out and push out the corners with scissor points. Fill the sachet with pot pourri, fold the seams in and over-sew the opening.

Filled with delicately perfumed pot pourri, this little sachet makes a lovely gift to scent a lingerie drawer or wardrobe. Each coloured cross on the chart above represents a single stitch, worked with two strands of thread, and each stitch covers one intersection of fabric.

Cut the fabric in half and work the design on one piece. Start from the centre of the design (the heart) and work outwards. To find the centre of your fabric, fold it in half and then in half again. Work two lines of running stitches along these folds to mark the centre point – these can be removed when the design has been stitched. Once you have finished the heart, stitch the blue flowers and then the green leaves and stems. Keep the back of your work free from knots and trim off any loose thread ends to prevent them from showing through to the right side.

Pansy handbag set

*This pansy-strewn glasses case and matching pen holder
will make a stylish birthday gift for a devoted correspondent.*

Pansy handbag set

YOU WILL NEED

- **31 × 45cm 12-gauge single canvas**
- **Paterna Persian yarn, one skein each of:**

Mid purple blue 343   340 Dark purple blue
Lavender 332   580 Dark blue
Dark plum 320   311 Grape
Violet 301   312 Lilac
Yellow 703   711 Light gold
Dark gold 700   716 Pale yellow
Dk spruce green 530   694 Pale green
Leaf green 692   690 Dark green

- **Two skeins each of:**

Kingfisher blue 582

- **Tapestry needle**
- **50 × 50cm lining/backing fabric**
- **1.2m narrow green twisted cord**
- **Large press stud**

This pretty matching set of a glasses case and pen holder is just right for handbag or briefcase. The rich colours of Persian yarn are perfect for the purples, mauves and golden yellows of the pansies and the deep kingfisher blue background is both attractive and practical. The glasses case has a flap which folds over at the front; it measures approximately 17cm by 9cm. The pen holder measures 7.5cm by 16cm.

PREPARING TO STITCH

The designs for the two items are shown on the colour charts opposite and on page 38. Each square on the charts equals one half cross-stitch. The colours of Persian yarn to use are shown on the key. In some parts of the design, the yarn colours have been combined in the needle for a subtle effect. These combinations of threads are also indicated on the keys on pages 37 and 38.

For the glasses case, cut a piece of canvas measuring 27cm by 31cm; for the pen holder, cut a piece of canvas 18cm × 26cm. Bind the

edges of both pieces with masking tape to prevent the yarn from catching on them as you stitch. If it does snag, it will become thin and will then not cover the canvas threads properly. Mark the horizontal and vertical centre lines on the canvas with a tacking thread and mark the centre lines of the chart in pencil. To keep the curved shape of the glasses case from distorting as you stitch, mount the canvas in a small slate frame. The pen holder, being smaller, will not distort as much; if it does, it can be pressed gently or stretched back into shape.

WORKING THE GLASSES CASE

Use two strands of the Persian yarn in the needle and work in half cross-stitch throughout. Secure your thread end at the back by working the first few stitches over it; finish off neatly by passing the needle through the last few stitches at the back. Complete each area

of colour before beginning the next and avoid carrying long strands of yarn across the back of the canvas as these will make the glasses case too bulky.

As the pansies are filled in with a lot of small areas of colour, you will find it helpful to thread up several needles with the different shades; you will then have each colour handy to work with as you need it. To prevent the colours you are not currently using from getting caught up in your stitching, take these threads to the right side of the canvas well away from the stitching area.

Begin stitching at the centre of the chart with the purple blue and lavender pansy, working the yellow and gold flower centre first and then moving on to the petals and leaves. Counting the squares on the chart carefully, work the other pansies and leaves surrounding the central pansy. Then fill in the background in kingfisher blue with dark blue

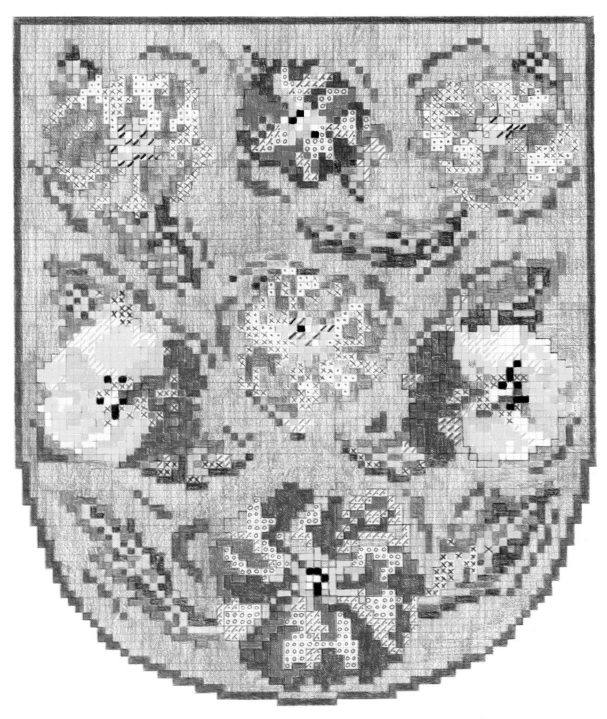

KEY

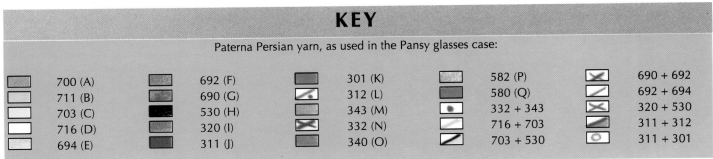

Paterna Persian yarn, as used in the Pansy glasses case:

700 (A)	692 (F)	301 (K)	582 (P)	690 + 692
711 (B)	690 (G)	312 (L)	580 (Q)	692 + 694
703 (C)	530 (H)	343 (M)	332 + 343	320 + 530
716 (D)	320 (I)	332 (N)	716 + 703	311 + 312
694 (E)	311 (J)	340 (O)	703 + 530	311 + 301

KEY

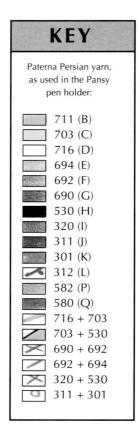

Paterna Persian yarn,
as used in the Pansy
pen holder:

▦	711 (B)
▦	703 (C)
▦	716 (D)
▦	694 (E)
▦	692 (F)
▦	690 (G)
■	530 (H)
▦	320 (I)
▦	311 (J)
▦	301 (K)
✎	312 (L)
▦	582 (P)
▦	580 (Q)
▱	716 + 703
◪	703 + 530
⊠	690 + 692
◩	692 + 694
⊠	320 + 530
▣	311 + 301

*Follow this chart to work the
Pansy pen holder to match
the glasses case on the
previous page. The key
above shows the colours of
Paterna Persian yarn to use
in the needle.*

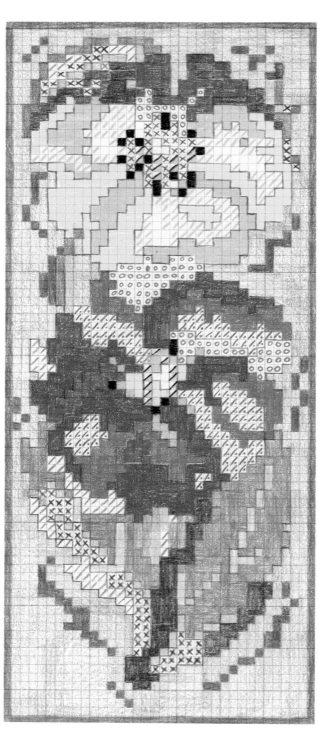

one of them to tuck in the ends of the twisted cord trim. Turn the case right side out.

Stitch the second pair of gussets to the lining in the same position as before. Turn under a 1cm seam allowance all round the lining fabric and insert it into the glasses case. Turn in the unstitched canvas and sew the lining to the needlepoint with small, neat slip stitches.

Trim the edges of the case with the twisted cord, neatening the ends by tucking them into the gap left between the canvas and the lining near the base of one of the gussets. Sew a press stud to the front flap with the corresponding part on the front section.

MAKING THE PEN HOLDER

Mark the centre of the canvas and the chart as for the glasses case. Using two strands of yarn in the needle, begin stitching centrally in half cross-stitch. Work the yellow and gold flower centre, then the plum, lavender and violet petals. Add the leaves, then stitch the mainly yellow pansy above it. Fill in the background last.

When the needlepoint is complete, restore it to shape if necessary by pressing gently with a steam iron. Trim the excess canvas to 1cm all round.

Cut a piece of backing fabric to match. With right sides facing, sew the backing fabric to the canvas with backstitch, leaving the top edge open. Turn through to the right side. Trim the edges with twisted cord, tucking the ends in at the top. Make the lining to match, insert it into the pen holder, turn under the raw edges at the top and secure it to the canvas and the backing with a neat slip stitch.

details. When the needlepoint is complete, remove it from the frame and check that the shape is symmetrical. If necessary, steam press gently from the back, pulling the canvas back into shape.

MAKING UP

Trim the excess canvas all round the glasses case, leaving a seam allowance of 1cm. The case now needs to be lined. Felt is a good choice for this, as it is soft and will protect your glasses. From the lining fabric, cut four gussets measuring 8cm by 5cm. Also cut an inner lining for the glasses case to the same shape as the finished canvas. With right sides facing, fold up the lower (straight) edge of the canvas by 8cm to form the front section. Insert two side gussets and pin in place, tapering the shape towards the bottom. Backstitch to the canvas, leaving a small gap near the base of

Pin cushion

This traditionally patterned needlepoint pin cushion would be
a welcome addition to any needlecrafter's work box.

Pin cushion

his fleur-de-lis design is worked in two strands of yarn throughout. Fold the canvas in quarters, mark the centre, then mount it in a small frame.

Each coloured square on the chart represents one half cross-stitch. First stitch the central petal in mustard, brown and yellow, then complete the fleur-de-lis motif. Then stitch the navy background around the fleur-de-lis and finish with the corners of the design.

Once the stitching is finished, stretch your canvas back into a perfect square. To back, stuff and finish the pin-cushion, follow the steps below.

YOU WILL NEED

- **10 × 10cm 12-gauge single canvas**
- **Paterna Persian yarn, one skein each of:**
    Yellow 727   571 Navy
    Brown 471   753 Mustard
    Pale yellow 715
- **Tapestry needle**
- **10 × 10cm polycotton backing fabric**
- **Polyester wadding**
- **Sewing needle and thread**

MAKING THE PIN CUSHION

Trim canvas to within four threads of the stitching. Place squarely on backing fabric, right sides together. Pin and tack around three edges, then backstitch together, keeping stitching abutting needlepoint closely.

Clip the canvas corners to within one canvas thread of the stitching and turn right side out. Fill the cushion with small pieces of polyester wadding until the cushion is plump but not bulging.

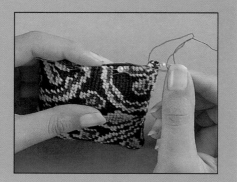

Turn back raw edges of backing and fold the canvas along the edge of the stitching. Pin together, then oversew using small, neat stitches in a thread to match the backing fabric.

Jewel brooch

Create a colourful and intricate alternative to real gems
with this cross-stitch jewel brooch.

Jewel brooch

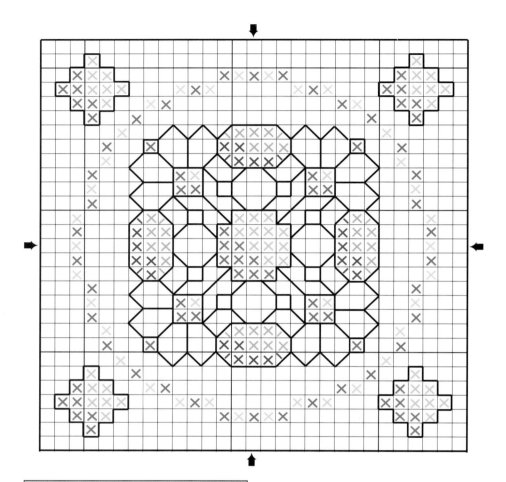

Neaten the back of the brooch by turning under the raw edges of the backing fabric and slip stitching the two pieces together.

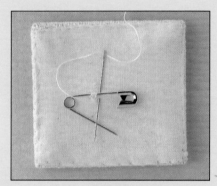

Attach the safety pin to the back of the brooch using the cream sewing thread and small oversewing stitches.

YOU WILL NEED

- **7 × 7cm 27-count cream evenweave fabric**
- **Madeira 6-stranded embroidery cotton, one skein each of:**

  Black 0714 Purple
  Crimson 0510 1404 Dark green
  Lilac 0713 1305 Pale green
  Dark red 0513
- **Tapestry needle**
- **7 × 7cm cream polycotton fabric**
- **Sharps needle**
- **Cream sewing thread**
- **Safety pin**

The fine lines of this detailed design resemble thin strands of silver often seen on antique jewellery. Each coloured cross on the chart above represents one stitch, using two strands of cotton worked over two threads of fabric.

Mark the centre points of the fabric and the chart, then begin stitching here using crimson (0510). The darker crosses on the rubies are worked in dark red (0513). The four amethysts are worked using purple (0714) and lilac (0713) and the large emeralds are worked in dark green (1404) and pale green (1305). The two-tone effect on each gem creates a sparkling lustre like cut stones. The ring of tiny emeralds around the central design is created by alternately placed dark and pale green crosses. Each 'stone' is outlined in backstitch, using one strand of black cotton. The fine interweaving black lines are also worked in black backstitching, as indicated by the solid black lines on chart. Keep the back of the work free from knots and trim off loose thread ends.

MAKING THE BROOCH

When you have finished stitching the design, cut a piece of stiff cardboard measuring 5cm square. Stretch the embroidery tightly over the card, making sure that the design is placed in the centre of the square, and secure the fabric on the back with four small pieces of masking tape. Tack down a small hem around each side of the polycotton, making sure it measures the same as the cardboard square. Slip stitch the polycotton on to the back of the worked area. This will cover the masking tape and any exposed cardboard. Finally, follow the steps above to attach the safety pin to the back of the brooch.

First home sampler

This beautiful sampler worked in easy cross-stitch would make a perfect wedding present.

First home sampler

YOU WILL NEED

- **40 × 50cm 14-count white aida fabric**
- **Madeira 6-stranded embroidery cotton, two skeins each of:**
  Rose pink 0505   1109 Blue green
  Emerald 1301
- **One skein each of:**
  Pale peach 2308   0403 Salmon
  Orange 2307   2209 Ochre
  Yellow 0109   1211 Pale green
  Olive 1408   1810 Charcoal
  White
- **Tapestry needle**
- **Frame and mount**

*T*he sampler is worked in cross-stitch on 14-count aida fabric. By adding the names of the newlyweds and the date of their wedding, you will make this special sampler unique.

PREPARING TO STITCH

Each cross-stitch is worked over one square of the aida fabric. Find the centre of your fabric by folding the material in half, first lengthways and then widthways. Mark the centre of the fabric with horizontal and vertical tacking stitches that can easily be removed later. Now calculate the central point of the chart on the photograph opposite and mark it in pencil.

You would normally begin stitching at the centre to ensure that the finished sampler is positioned in the middle of the fabric, with opposite seams of identical widths. But in this case the centre is just below where you will

be stitching the date. It is best to leave the letters and numbers until the end so that you can position them correctly within the context of the surrounding stitching.

Work with the sampler stretched taut on a hoop or a frame. Each single cross-stitch is worked with a needle threaded with two

The colours selected for the sampler (above) are a particularly attractive combination of pinks, browns and greens. Arrange samples on a card and label them for easy reference as you sew.

KEY

Madeira 6-stranded embroidery cotton, as used in the Sampler:

A	0505	**G**	1211
B	2308	**H**	1109
C	0403	**I**	1301
D	2307	**K**	1408
E	2209	**L**	1810
F	0109	**M**	White

strands of embroidery cotton. The chart photograph on page 45 has been reproduced large enough for you to count stitches for each motif, and the key and swatches (page 44) make it easy to select the colours.

Begin by working the roof of the house in two strands of ochre (2209), followed by the front hedge and trees. Work the ribbon and bells, then the bride and groom, the two four-leaf clovers and the hearts. Complete this section by working the surrounding border. Stitch the two little dogs, then move up to

work the motifs above the lettering. Count carefully to position the upper motifs and borders so that you have space to work the names and date. Work the bowl of fruit, then the border in two shades of green, followed

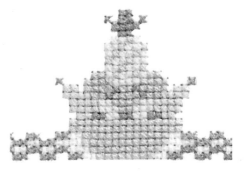

by the two rose bushes, the hearts and the two borders above. Finally, enclose the whole piece with a border of blue green, ochre, pale peach and white.

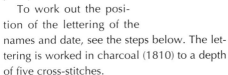

To work out the position of the lettering of the names and date, see the steps below. The lettering is worked in charcoal (1810) to a depth of five cross-stitches.

When the embroidery is completed, press it lightly on the wrong side. Mount and frame the sampler as you wish.

HOW TO PLAN STITCHED LETTERING

1 Use the sample alphabet above to spell out the names of the couple on graph paper, allowing one clear space between each of the letters and two clear spaces between each word.

2 Count the number of graph paper squares which the names and spaces have taken and divide it in half. Mark the exact halfway point of the lettering on the graph paper with a line.

3 Match the centre point of the lettering to the vertical centre line of the stitched sampler. Stitch from the centre outwards, following your graph paper plan. Repeat for the date below the names.

Violet bed linen

Decorated with pretty violets in delicate shades of purple and green, this sheet and matching pillowcase would make an attractive gift for a bride.

YOU WILL NEED

- **Plain cotton percale sheet and pillowcase**
- **50 × 50cm 10-count waste canvas**
- **Madeira 6-stranded embroidery cotton, one skein each of:**
     Yellow 0107   0711 Pale lilac
     Mid violet 0712
- **Two skeins each of:**
  Dark violet 0805   1509 Pale green
     Dark green 1312
- **Three skeins of:**
     Mid green 1401
- **Crewel needle**
- **Sewing thread**

Violet bed linen

What could be more luxurious and individual than putting special designs on a set of bed linen? In this matching set, the delicate touch of trailing violets adds colour and charm to crisp, ivory cotton. This set of matching pillowcase and sheet would make a unique present for a friend or relative. The design, made up of small crosses which accentuate the realistic light and shade effect, has been worked in cross-stitch through waste canvas using stranded embroidery cotton.

WASTE CANVAS

The use of waste canvas enables you to work counted cross-stitch on fabrics which have threads too fine to be counted, such as cotton. The stiffened canvas is available by the metre in various thread counts to the inch. On 10-count, as recommended, the sheet design will measure 31 × 8.5cm, and the pillowcase 25 × 17cm. If you require a smaller finished result, choose a finer canvas – a 12-count canvas will produce a sheet design 23 × 7.5cm, and 22 × 14cm on the pillowcase. The reverse also applies – if you want a larger design, choose a gauge of waste canvas with fewer stitches to the inch.

For this bed-linen, a fairly coarse canvas with ten threads to the inch has been chosen since the violets design would be lost on such a large area if the stitching was too delicate. The pillowcase and the sheet are ivory, of standard size, and made of pure cotton.

WORKING THE PILLOWCASE

To work the pillowcase, cut a piece of waste canvas measuring 31 × 24cm. Position the canvas squarely in the corner of the pillowcase, 5cm from the long edge and 9.5cm from the short edge. Tack firmly in place using sewing thread through one layer of the pillowcase. Make sure that the threads of the waste

To work the pillowcase corner design, follow the illustration centre right. The charts for the sheet are shown separately. To stitch the left-hand side of the sheet, follow the illustration on the left. The chart for the right-hand side of the sheet is shown far right. Use the key provided as a guide to colours.

canvas are parallel to those of the pillowcase. Tack the canvas all round the edge and at intervals vertically and horizontally in both directions to secure it to the fabric (see Preparing the pillowcase on page 50 for details).

Mark the centre of the waste canvas square with lines of tacking and the centre point of the chart in pencil. Beginning at the centre, work the design in cross-stitch, stitching through both the canvas holes and the cotton, using three strands of thread. Work cross-stitch in the usual way, counting the threads of the waste canvas as you go. Use the cross-stitch chart as a guide to colours. One square on the chart represents one complete cross-stitch. Remove tacking threads once they have been covered by cross-stitches.

REMOVING THE CANVAS

When you have completed the violet design, remove all remaining tacking threads which are holding the waste canvas in place. Moisten the finished work with a damp, clean cloth to soften the waste canvas and carefully remove the threads, easing them from underneath the stitches out one at a time, first in one direction and then in the other. Try using tweezers to pull out stubborn threads. Allow the work to dry slightly and then using a

---

PRACTICAL

When moving the hoop to a new area of your work, it is a good idea to press the canvas with a dry iron before placing it back in the hoop again. This will iron out the crumples left by the hoop and ensure that the waste canvas continues to lie flat against the cotton fabric. Never use a steam setting when ironing waste canvas – this will slightly dampen and therefore soften the waste canvas threads. If the threads become soft, it will be very difficult to stitch over them without catching them and you may well have to start all over again.

POINTS

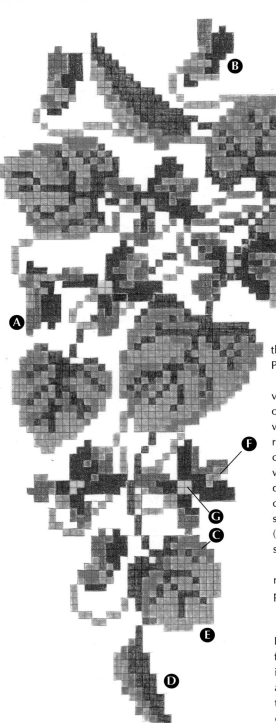

the sheet in a corresponding position (see Preparing the sheet on page 50).

Mark the centre of each strip of waste canvas with lines of tacking and the centre of side of the chart in pencil. Following the chart, work the sheet design (shown here on the right) on the left-hand side of the sheet in cross-stitch using three strands of thread. As with the pillowcase, begin in the centre of the design and work your stitches through the canvas holes and the cotton fabric, making small, neat crosses. Work the reversed design (shown opposite) on the right-hand side of the sheet top in the same way.

When all the embroidery is complete, moisten and remove the canvas threads and press on the wrong side as for the pillowcase.

REVERSING A CHART

If you needed to reverse a chart yourself, say for the top left-hand corner of a pillowcase, it is very easy to do. The simplest way to reverse a design is to copy the cross-stitch chart on tracing paper printed with a graph grid, using coloured pencils or felt-tipped pens. Tape the tracing paper down while you copy the design to stop it from moving. When you have traced all the design, remove the tape and turn the tracing paper over; the design will show through clearly in reverse.

warm, dry iron, press on the wrong side, with the right side lying on a soft, clean towel.

STITCHING THE SHEET

Before you start stitching, measure the top of the sheet in both directions to find the centre and mark it with a piece of tacking thread. Cut out two pieces of waste canvas each measuring 12 × 35cm. Tack one piece firmly to the right-hand side of the sheet, 3cm from the centre of the sheet and 2.5cm from the border hem stitching, so the finished design sits square to the fabric threads. Tack the second piece of waste canvas on to the other side of

KEY

Madeira 6-stranded embroidery cotton, as used on the Violet bed linen:

Ⓐ	Mid violet (0712)	Ⓔ	Pale green (1509)
Ⓑ	Dk violet (0805)	Ⓕ	Pale lilac (0711)
Ⓒ	Mid green (1401)	Ⓖ	Yellow (0107)
Ⓓ	Dark green (1312)		

PREPARING THE PILLOWCASE

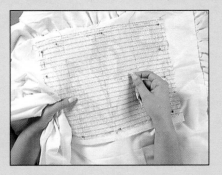

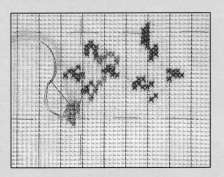

1 Cut out a piece of waste canvas measuring 31 × 24cm. It makes sense to cut out the two pieces for the sheet, each 12 x 35cm, at this stage too.

2 Position and pin canvas on top layer of pillowcase, lining up vertical threads with those of the fabric. Tack round edges and at intervals across and down. Remove pins.

3 Start stitching in cross-stitch from the central point of the chart. Begin working in mid violet (0712), then move on to mid green (1401).

PREPARING THE SHEET

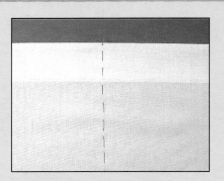

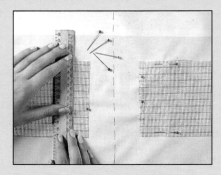

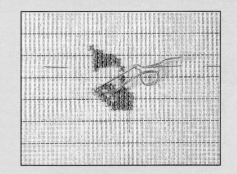

1 Measure across the sheet top to find and mark centre point. Using sewing thread, make a line of running stitches downwards to indicate the centre line.

2 Position and pin canvas on one side, square to sheet top and centre line. Pin second piece of canvas the same distance from centre and top to mirror the first.

3 Start stitching from the centre of the chart. First work pale areas of central leaf in cross-stitch using mid green (1401).

fine stitching

When stitching large areas of colour in counted cross-stitch, work the crosses in rows, instead of individually, wherever possible (see page 34). This method produces smoother stitches because it is worked with an even tension, so the thread lies flatter against the fabric.

To achieve the effect of light and shade in a professional way, you can vary the direction of the top diagonals of your stitches so that when the light catches the finished work, the result will be a textured appearance. This technique will accentuate the shading on the leaves.

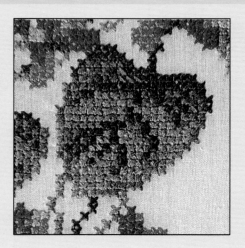

Guest towels

*Pretty hand towels in different cross-stitch designs will look
fresh and crisp in a friend's new home.*

Guest towels

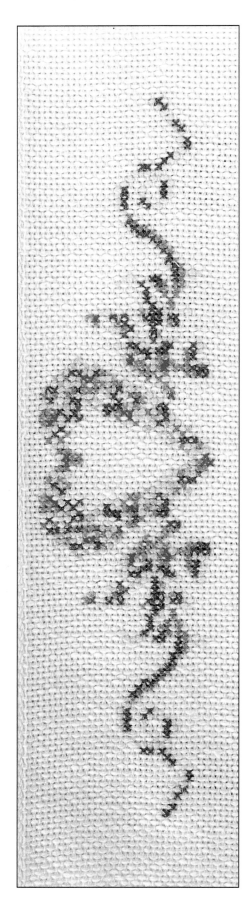

Soft terry cloth 'fingertip' towels are available in assorted pastel shades, and we have chosen a light cream for these two lovely floral designs.

Before you start stitching, use the keys on this and the next page to sort your embroidery cottons so that you have the right shades for each design – some colours are common to both. Where there are several shades of one colour it is helpful to label them with the letter from the key and the symbol representing that colour on the charts on page 87. Now find the centre of the evenweave stitching area on each of the towels and mark it with a row of running stitches which you can remove later.

Where you separate strands of cotton, you get a smoother result if you take out individual strands and put them back together than if you simply pull off two threads at a time. Make sure, especially as you are working with a very scattered pattern for this design, that the first diagonal of your cross-stitches always lies in the same direction.

HEART DESIGN

Stretch the centre of the evenweave stitching area in an embroidery hoop before you start stitching. Working in two strands of cotton throughout this design, start with the centre top of the heart with the two stitches in pale pink (0503) on the central flower. These should fall one either side of your centre line, over the seventh fabric intersection from the top of the border area.

Since there are no large blocks of one colour in the heart design, it is a good idea to work all the stitches of one shade, such as the pale pink, in one small area, filling in the other colours as you go, positioning them in relation to the existing stitches. Work round the heart design to the right and left of the first two pink 'anchor' stitches. Complete the small flower at the centre top and add the foliage around it.

With the heart complete, start on one of the clusters of flowers and foliage to the side of the heart. The dull green (1213) is a good colour on which to build up the pattern – just position your first stitches carefully in relation to the stitching on the heart.

When you have filled in the main flowers and buds, continue down the trails of greenery in mid green (1303), then in dull green and mint (1208). Mirror this design on the other side of the heart in the same way.

It is better to finish off the thread of each colour and start afresh in another area rather than leave long lengths of cotton which will

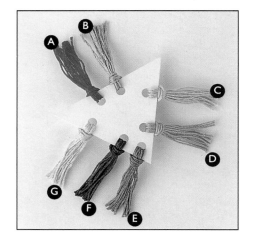

show through on the right side. Threads taken from one area to another across the back of the work may become snagged during use, so although it may take longer, it is worth finishing off and starting again to avoid loops on the back of the work.

LOOSE ENDS

When you have finished all the stitching, remove the towel from the hoop and check the back of the work. It is important, since the towels will have to stand up to normal use, that you make sure that all the loose ends on the reverse are neatly worked in and trimmed so that the back of the towel is neat and not likely to unravel. Now sort the threads which are common to both designs so that they are correctly labelled to use for the second towel. As in the first towel, the cross-stitching is all worked using two strands of thread – only the dark green lines worked in Holbein stitch (see page 108) are worked using just one strand of

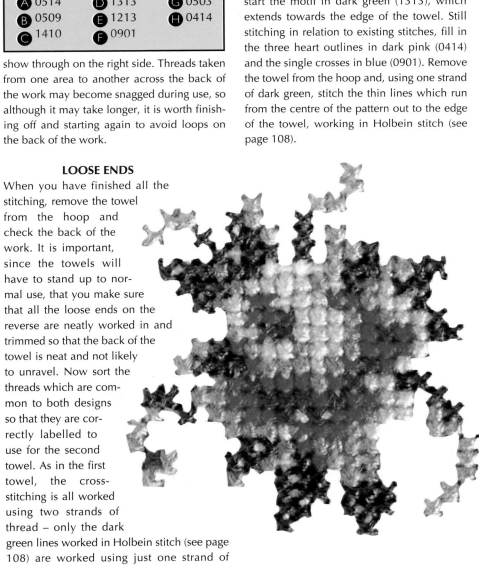

thread. Stretch the fabric in an embroidery hoop so that you can stitch to one side of the marked centre line.

ROSE DESIGN

As there is no stitching across the line down the centre of the evenweave area, begin with the foliage in lime (1410) at the centre top of the pattern. The stitch nearest the centre in the cluster of three should fall on the fourth fabric intersection to the left (or right) of the centre line, nine intersections down from the top of the stitching area. Continue that side of the design, completing the leaves in three shades of green, then progressing to the large rose. See the steps on page 54 for stitching details.

MIRROR DESIGN

Fill in all the greenery around the rose, then start the motif in dark green (1313), which extends towards the edge of the towel. Still stitching in relation to existing stitches, fill in the three heart outlines in dark pink (0414) and the single crosses in blue (0901). Remove the towel from the hoop and, using one strand of dark green, stitch the thin lines which run from the centre of the pattern out to the edge of the towel, working in Holbein stitch (see page 108).

STITCHING DETAILS

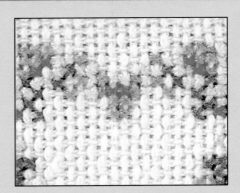  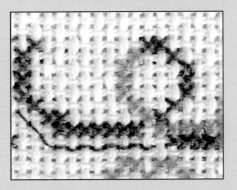

The first stitches to work on the heart design are the two pale pink crosses, positioned one either side of the centre of the stitching area. From this point, work to right and left to fill in the heart shape.

The shades of red and pink used for the main rose motif tend to blend together – well labelled threads and careful following of the charts will ensure that you achieve the right effect of light and dark.

Work the defining lines on the rose towel in Holbein or backstitch, using just one strand of dark green embroidery cotton. Keep the tension even, as the soft evenweave fabric can distort when it is not in a hoop.

Once you have completed one half of the design, remove the towel from the hoop and reposition it to stitch the other side.

As with the heart design, make sure that all the stitching is well secured on the back – and your two guest towels are ready to give.

VERSATILE COLOURS

The basic patterns on the two towels would lend themselves very well to interpretation in different shades to suit the colour scheme of a bathroom.

bright ideas

Both the rose and heart designs work well as borders for household linens other than towels.

Worked on 14-count aida ribbon, either motif would look perfect for a pair of curtain tiebacks.

The same designs could be used to trim a make-up bag, or to decorate the ends of a table runner, with, perhaps, small round table mats with a single heart motif in the centre to complete the set.

Similarly, working on a firm evenweave fabric such as hardanger, you could repeat the designs along a border for a bathroom blind as a perfect complement to the guest towels.

Pinks and minty greens are a classic colour combination, but if you wanted to produce a sunnier effect, you could use a combination of peach, orange and apricot colours, altering the bright greens to more muted shades of sage and grey-green.

To achieve the same sort of effect in a different colour scheme, simply select colours of a comparable tone to those used here. For example, for the heart design, in place of the pale pink, try a light apricot such as Madeira colour number 0304, with darker shades 0301 and 0206, and use greens 1602, 1603 and 1512, and a light yellow such as 0111 in place of the pale blue. To carry the same

colour scheme over to the heart design, use the common colours as in the main instructions, and complete the thread selection using chestnut 0313 in place of the maroon, ochre 0309 instead of the dark red and greens 1501 and 1514.

In the same way, you can ring the changes with the towels themselves. You can buy suitable 'fingertip' towels in different pastel shades but, because they are pure cotton, the towels take dye very well. Very strong dark colours would not be suitable for the colourways used here – but with a different set of threads in more vibrant colours, the possibilities are endless.

Wedding bookmark

With embroidered doves and ribbons, this traditional cross-stitch
bookmark will make a perfect gift for a special day.

Wedding bookmark

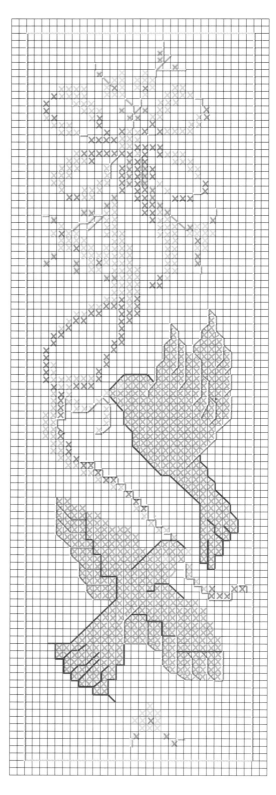

A wedding is probably the most important day in a couple's life and what better way to commemorate it than with this pretty cross-stitch bookmark worked on 14-count white aida fabric in shades of blue, pink, grey, yellow and green embroidery cotton?

STARTING TO STITCH

Following the chart on the left, work the design in cross-stitch using two strands of cotton throughout. Find the centre of the fabric by folding it in half and then in half again. Mark the centre lines with tacking which can be worked over and then removed when the design is complete.

Once you have embroidered all the motifs in cross-stitch, outline where indicated on the chart using Holbein or backstitch (see page 108). Work round the outer birds' wings using dark pink and the inner bodies using dark grey. Outline the thin trailing ribbon using dark blue and dark pink and work the stems using green.

To complete the bookmark, stitch the border using dark pink for the sides and pale pink for the top and bottom.

FINISHING TOUCHES

Using a small, sharp pair of embroidery scissors, carefully cut around the bookmark, leaving a border two squares deep. Remove the threads up to the stitched border carefully to create a fringed edging, leaving one or two threads of the aida fabric outside the stitching.

YOU WILL NEED

- **6.25 × 20cm 14-count white aida fabric**

- **Madeira 6-stranded embroidery cotton, one skein each of:**

Dark grey 1801	1805 Grey
Pale pink 0503	0505 Dark pink
Light blue 0908	0910 Dark blue
Green 1211	0110 Yellow

- **Tapestry needle**

New baby card

Celebrate the arrival of a new addition by working this charming
little card in cross-stitch and adding a name and date.

New baby card

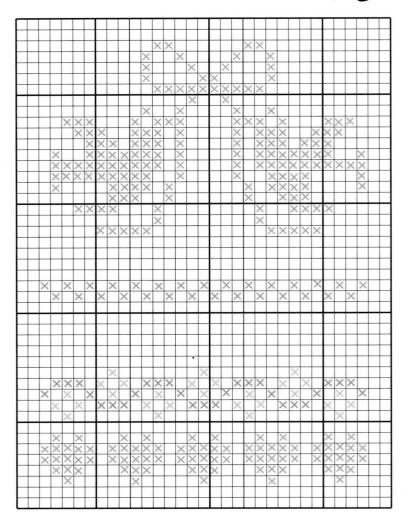

*I*t is always exciting when a new baby is born, so make the occasion even more special by stitching a congratulations card with the child's name and date of birth. The card is worked in the pastel shades appropriate for tiny babies and can be adapted to tradition for a boy or a girl by simply switching the pink and blue cottons.

WORKING THE CARD

Mark the centre of the fabric by folding it and tacking the lines. The design is symmetrical and simple to work. Use the chart to position your coloured stitches correctly. Each square on the chart represents one stitch on the fabric and every cross-stitch is worked using two strands of cotton in the needle.

PERSONAL TOUCH

When you have finished the cross-stitches, work the baby's date of birth in the space provided between the ribbon-carrying birds and the central pink line of stitching. Work the baby's name underneath the central line, using the photograph to help you position it (see also page 46). The numerals and letters are worked in backstitch using one strand of cotton. An alphabet and the outlines for the numbers are given on page 125.

To make up the card, spread fabric glue sparingly over the central section of the card and lay it over your stitching, positioning the design in the centre of the aperture, and press down firmly (see also page 32).

bright idea

To make this card traditional for a baby girl, simply change the colours used to work certain areas of the design. On the boy's version, the bow, the name and the lower row of hearts are worked in blue. For the girl's version, work these in pink. Then use the blue to work the band of alternate cross-stitches below the date. All the other colours in the design are the same. Add your chosen name and date following the chart on page 46 or page 125.

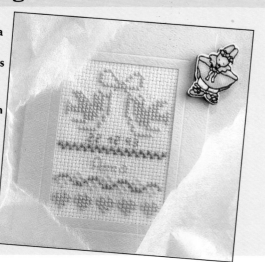

Baby blanket

Cosy and cute, this irresistible cot blanket, worked in cross-stitch, features an adorable baby teddy bear who is ready for bed.

YOU WILL NEED

- **19-count evenweave fringed baby blanket**

- **Madeira 6-stranded embroidery cotton, three skeins each of:**
  Sky blue 0910 1002 Pale blue

- **Two skeins each of:**
  Mid pink 0607 White

- **One skein each of:**
  Light green 1701   2307 Gold
  Butterscotch 2013   2001 Pale grey
  Pale yellow 0102   1710 Blue grey
  Creamy yellow 2014   2003 Dark brown
  Coffee 2009   1802 Mid grey
  Mid yellow 0112   0501 Pale pink
  Black

- **Tapestry needle**

- **4.5m mid blue ribbon, 4mm wide**

Baby blanket

What baby could resist snuggling up under this cosy cot blanket at bedtime? The blanket has been decorated with a cuddly teddy bear who is dressed in his pyjamas and ready for bed. The colours are soft and muted to match any nursery or bedroom decor. Surrounded by pink hearts and 'sweet dreams', this teddy looks absolutely adorable.

Instead of working on a purchased baby blanket, you could choose any fabric you like and work cross-stitch using 10-count waste canvas (see page 50). Tack the waste canvas to your fabric and work your stitches as normal. Before you start to stitch, prepare the materials you will need in advance. In good daylight, identify and label the threads with the corresponding colour and symbol as used on the chart.

The charts for the blanket appear on pages 90–1; each symbol represents one colour. The

design is worked in cross-stitch using three strands of thread; outlines are worked in back-stitch using one strand. Half cross-stitch and three-quarter cross-stitch have both been used in places for shading. To position the design on the fabric, fold the fabric in half and in half again and mark the centre with lines of tacking. Then, on the chart, follow the black arrows on the diagram and mark the centre with a pencil.

STARTING TO STITCH

Each square on the charts on pages 90–1 represents one cross-stitch; one stitch should be worked over two fabric threads and up two fabric threads using three strands in the needle. To start stitching, work the centre stitch of the design, using blue grey (1710), on the centre threads of the fabric. Hold the end of the thread against the back of the fabric and work your first few stitches over it to secure

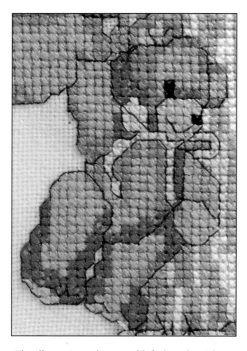

The illustrations above and left show how the detailed shading is achieved. Use these and the illustration on the right as a colour reference when stitching. The key opposite will help you to identify the colours.

the thread. Continue in cross-stitch, following the symbol chart and using the key opposite as a guide to the colours.

When you have completed the blue grey in the pyjamas, move on to stitch the pale blue stripes (1002) and then the white. To start a new colour, pass the needle under a few stitches on the back of the work to secure the thread and continue. Fill in the collar and the cuffs using sky blue (0910). Work one colour area at a time and count your stitches carefully as you go. Then add the pyjama buttons and motif using mid pink (0607), pale pink (0501), and white. Fill in the pale grey shaded areas to complete the pyjamas.

KEY

Madeira 6-stranded embroidery cotton, as used on the Baby blanket:

White		Pale yellow 0102	
Pale pink 0501		Mid yellow 0112	
Mid pink 0607		Pale blue 1002	
Light green 1701		Sky blue 0910	
Blue grey 1710		Pale grey 2001	
Cream 2014		Mid grey 1802	
Gold 2307		Butterscotch 2013	
Dk brown 2003		Coffee 2009	
Black			

STITCHING THE BEAR

Once the pyjamas have been completed, stitch the teddy bear's hands using butter-scotch (2013) and gold (2307). Try to keep the tension of your stitches even and make sure the top diagonals of your stitches lie in the same direction. Work the bear's head and ears in the same two colours. Add shading where indicated on the chart using coffee (2009). Do not carry the thread too far across the back of the work, especially when using darker colours, as the thread might show through on the front.

Fill in the light areas on teddy's muzzle and ears in creamy yellow (2014) and stitch his features in sky blue and black. As you stitch, your embroidery cotton will probably become twisted – every so often, let the needle fall from your hand to allow the thread to unwind itself before you resume.

Next work the small teddy bear in butter-scotch, gold and coffee. Fill in the light areas using creamy yellow and the features in black. His bow tie is worked in mid pink. Then stitch the teddy's own blanket in pale yellow (0102) and add the shading using mid yellow (0112). The shading under the bear is worked in mid grey (1802) using half cross-stitch to give a different texture.

FINISHING TOUCHES

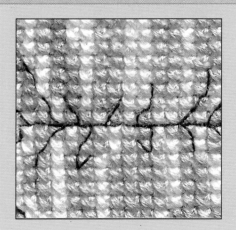

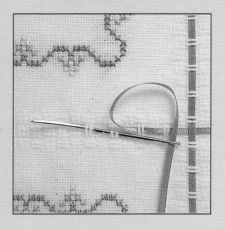

The detail on the teddy bear's ankles is simply worked in backstitch. Using one strand of coffee (2009), work backstitch horizontally and diagonally on top of the crosses over two threads to produce a thin line and give the effect of gathers.

To give the teddy bear's ears a more natural shape, three-quarter cross-stitches have been worked across the corner in gold (2307). The whole of the shape has then been outlined using one strand of coffee (2009), with extra detail added to the ears.

A delicate powder blue ribbon, or pale pink for a baby girl, will add the finishing touch to your baby blanket. Thread the ribbon through a bodkin or large tapestry needle and weave it in and out of the woven threads of the border as above.

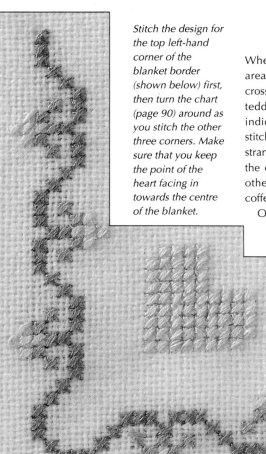

Stitch the design for the top left-hand corner of the blanket border (shown below) first, then turn the chart (page 90) around as you stitch the other three corners. Make sure that you keep the point of the heart facing in towards the centre of the blanket.

OUTLINE STITCHES

When you have filled in the main colour areas of the design in cross-stitch and half cross-stitch, you can add the fine details to the teddy bear. Outline the shapes where indicated in backstitch, working all outline stitches over two fabric threads. Using three strands of black thread, outline the pupils of the eyes, the nose and the mouth. Work all other outline stitches using one strand of coffee (2009).

Once the central motif is complete, move on to the floral border inside the woven edge of the blanket. The floral border motif is shown on a separate chart on page 90 – the chart for the upper left-hand corner has been supplied. When you have stitched this corner, turn the chart round to complete the remaining corners, stitching each corner with the point

of the heart facing the blanket. You will also find a small diagram of the whole blanket, showing how to position the borders.

Either of the alphabet and number charts given on pages 46 and 125 will allow you to personalise your blanket.

When the stitching is complete, weave the narrow ribbon through the border as shown in the steps above. Trim the ends of the ribbon so that they are even with the edge of the fringe, and your blanket is ready to present to a special baby.

Nursery rhyme quilt

The characters from five favourite nursery tales are worked
in cross-stitch on this delightful cot quilt.

Nursery rhyme quilt

The bright colours and pretty pictures on this cross-stitch quilt will delight even the youngest child. It features five well-known nursery rhymes and stories: Little Red Riding Hood, Jack and Jill, Goldilocks and the Three Bears, Little Miss Muffet and Humpty Dumpty. As well as being the focal point of the nursery bedding, the quilt will also start off many a bedtime story.

The five panels, are worked on aida fabric, and are separated by panels on broderie anglaise fabric and padded with washable polyester wadding. The quilt is backed with polycotton, so it is practical as well as attractive. Quilting is worked around each panel to secure all the layers together and the edge is finished off with a broderie anglaise frill. The completed quilt measures approximately 53 × 67cm without the frill and each cross-stitch panel measures 17.5 × 22.5cm.

For a brighter quilt, use a pastel coloured broderie anglaise fabric and frill, picking a colour that is featured in one of the panels. Alternatively use a plain polycotton fabric for the panels and trim the design with a frill made by folding a long strip of the fabric in half widthways.

MAKING THE PANELS

For each of the five panels cut a piece of aida fabric measuring 25cm × 30cm. Bind the raw edges with masking tape to prevent them from fraying as you work the embroidery. To help you position the designs correctly on the fabric, mark the centre horizontal and vertical lines with tacking stitches. Mount the fabric in an embroidery hoop or frame if you wish.

The charts for the designs are shown beginning on page 94; each symbol represents one cross-stitch and the solid lines on some of the charts represent the backstitching. The key on each chart shows you which colour of stranded cotton to use for each symbol.

Mark the centre point of the chart in pencil and begin stitching here, working out towards the edges in blocks of colour. Finish off each area of colour before beginning the next, and do not take

long strands of the cotton across the back of the work when moving from one part of the picture to another, as these may show through on the right side. Use two strands of cotton in the needle throughout, and make sure that the top part of each cross slopes in the same direction or the finished embroidery will have an uneven appearance. To help you remember in which direction to work the cross-stitches, work a large cross in one corner of the panel, over three or

Goldilocks and the three bears are featured in the bottom right-hand corner of the quilt. Their pretty cottage with its blue roof has a meandering path and flower-strewn lawn in front of it.

YOU WILL NEED

- **60 × 100cm 14-count white aida fabric**
- **Madeira 6-stranded embroidery cotton, one skein each of:**

Light green 1310	1307 Lime green
Jade green 1213	1314 Dark green
Dark brown 2007	2311 Pinky brown
Copper brown 2009	2211 Gold
Yellow 0108	0112 Pale yellow
Beige 2013	0502 Pale pink
Flesh 0305	0303 Dark flesh
Bright blue 0911	1712 Slate blue
Pale blue 0907	1709 Pale grey
Grey 1808	0903 Violet
Purple 0713	0708 Cyclamen pink
Red 0210	0513 Dark red

- **Tapestry needle**
- **60 × 70cm white broderie anglaise fabric**
- **80 × 125cm white polycotton**
- **60 × 75cm light-weight polyester wadding**
- **2.6m pre-gathered broderie anglaise frill, 14cm wide**
- **Sewing needle and thread**

four holes of the aida fabric. If you work each leg of the cross-stitch in different colours, there can be no confusion. For all the panels, work the picture before adding the double border.

PANEL 1: LITTLE MISS MUFFET

This panel is shown in the top left-hand corner of the quilt. Begin stitching the panel in the centre at the bow in Little Miss Muffet's hair, then work down to her hair itself and her face. Continue with her apron and dress, then add her hands and feet. Fill in the 'tuffet' and the flower-strewn grass in the foreground, and then work the bowl and the spoon. Finish off the picture by working the tree on the right-hand side, including the spider whose legs and dangling thread are worked in backstitch. Finish the panel by working the border.

PANEL 2: JACK AND JILL

This popular child's rhyme is pictured in the top right-hand corner of the quilt. Start stitching at the central tuft of grass, moving on to the bush with Jack falling into it. Fill in the hill in the background, adding the well at the top. The well handle is worked in backstitch. Then stitch Jill, starting with her top shoe and moving across to her striped stocking and her dress. Add her other shoe and stocking, then

Little Miss Muffet sat on a tuffet, eating her curds and whey. Along came a spider and sat down beside her and frightened Miss Muffet away.

her face and hands. Finish by working the other patches of grass, the pink flowers and the bucket. Outline the panel with the border.

PANEL 3: HUMPTY DUMPTY

The story of Humpty Dumpty's demise is familiar to all children and he is shown in the central panel on the quilt. Begin by stitching Humpty's bow tie, then his shirt, belt, trousers and shoes. Add his face and features, working his eyebrows and nose in backstitch. Then

stitch the bricks in the wall and the flowers growing in front of it. Finish the picture by working the clouds in the sky. Add the double border around the panel to complete it.

PANEL 4: LITTLE RED RIDING HOOD

The story of Little Red Riding Hood and the Big Bad Wolf is a favourite with children of all ages and this panel, shown in the bottom left-hand corner of the quilt, depicts her trotting off to visit her grandmother. Begin by stitching Little Red Riding Hood's face, then her hair and cloak. Add her hands, with the bunch of flowers and the basket, and her feet. Then work the path and the flowers in the foreground, followed by tree trunks and leaves.

PANEL 5: GOLDILOCKS AND THE THREE BEARS

The best place to begin is with the bush next to the house. Then work the house; the stems of the rambling rose around the door are worked in backstitch. Add the figure of Goldilocks on the right of the house. Next stitch the path and the surrounding grass and

bright idea

Any of these traditional panels could be used on their own as a framed picture; or make all five for an unusual series. Here we have used the Humpty Dumpty panel which is in the centre of the quilt.

To make a picture, look at the chart given for the design of your choice on pages 94–9 and buy one skein of each colour stated for it in the key. If you want to make a smaller picture, omit the double cross-stitch border that frames the panel. Add a contrast mount and frame.

flowers. Finally work the three bears in the foreground.

MAKING UP THE QUILT

Press the panels from the back over a padded surface so as not to flatten the stitches. Trim the fabric to 1.5cm all around the outer frame of each panel. Cut out four panels from the broderie anglaise fabric to the same size.

Tack the top two embroidered panels to either side of a broderie anglaise panel, in the order shown in the photograph. Make sure you leave one row of aida squares all around the edge of the frame of each embroidered panel. Machine stitch the seams. Make two more strips in the same way, alternating the cross-stitched panels with the broderie anglaise ones as in the photograph. Then tack and machine stitch the three strips together. When you join the panels, take care that the seam lines match (see below).

Cut two pieces of polycotton fabric, each 56cm by 70cm; one is to line the back of the embroidered panels and the other to back the whole quilt. Also cut a piece of wadding measuring 56 × 70cm. Place the wadding on a flat surface and lay the polyester lining and then the embroidered panels over the top. Pin and tack all the layers together around each rectangle and then pin and tack all around the edge. Tack the broderie anglaise frill around

the edge of the embroidered quilt top, raw edges aligning.

With right sides facing, pin and tack the backing fabric to the quilt with a 1.5cm seam allowance and machine stitch around the edge, leaving an opening to turn it through. Clip the corners and trim away excess wadding. Turn the quilt through and sew up the opening with slip stitch. To secure the layers together, quilt around each panel by working small, neat running stitches around the edge. Alternatively, you could quilt the panels by machine.

Jack and Jill went up the hill to fetch a pail of water; Jack fell down and broke his crown and Jill came tumbling after.

Little Red Riding Hood carries a basket and a bunch of flowers as she trots through the woods to visit her grandmother.

WHAT WENT WRONG?

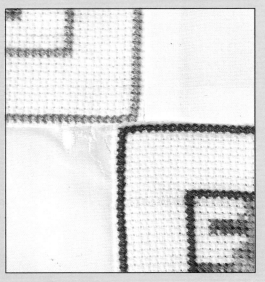

When you are joining the panels together in their strips of three, it is very important to make sure that the seam lines match exactly.

To do this, place the strips together with right sides facing and insert the point of a pin first through one panel seam, then through the same seam on the panel underneath. Bring the pin back through to the wrong side of the upper strip in the same way. The seams will then align perfectly. If you do not do this, the seams will have a stepped and untidy appearance as shown in the picture on the right.

Aesop's fables

These small cross-stitch pictures illustrate three of the much-loved stories written by Aesop around 600 B.C.

Aesop's fables

Most people probably remember at least one or two of Aesop's fables from their childhood – those little tales with a moral at the end, often featuring animals. These delightful cross-stitch panels show three of the better-known ones: *The Fox and the Crow*, *The Hare and the Tortoise*, and *The Peacock and the Crane*. They are designed to look rather like old-fashioned book illustrations with a decorative border around each one, and they would make a beautiful gift for a special child. Each picture measures 13cm by 17cm before framing. Choose a simple frame and a cream mount or leave an aida border on all four edges.

PREPARING TO STITCH

The three designs are shown as black-and-white charts on page 92. Each symbol equals one cross-stitch and the key shows you which

"…and the bird opened her beak…and as she did so, the piece of cheese fell…" The fox with its open, expectant mouth is worked in shades of rust and grey.

colour to use for each symbol. Before you begin stitching, oversew the raw edges of the aida fabric or bind them with masking tape to prevent them from fraying. Fold the fabric lightly in half each way and mark the centre lines with tacking which can be worked over and then removed when the design is complete. Mark the centre lines of your chosen chart in the same way in pencil.

STITCHING THE DESIGNS

Stretch the fabric in an embroidery hoop if you wish, as this will help you to keep an even tension and produce a more professional-looking result. Using two strands of cotton in the needle, begin stitching centrally, counting the coloured squares on the chart carefully. Use lengths of thread no more than 45cm long, so that they do not tangle or begin to wear thin. To start off neatly, leave a short length of cotton at the back and work the first few cross-stitches over it; to finish off, pass the needle under the last few stitches worked at the back and then cut off the thread end very short. In this way, no trailing ends will get caught up in subsequent stitching and risk being pulled through to the front.

Work one area of colour at a time and finish it off before beginning the next. Remember not to take lengths of thread across the back of the work from one area of the design to another, as these will show through at the front and may get tangled up with other parts of your stitching.

THE FOX AND THE CROW

In this fable, the fox wants the piece of cheese which the crow has in its beak. To trick the bird into letting it drop, the fox praises its singing voice until the crow is persuaded to open its beak to try a song. The cheese falls into the waiting mouth of the triumphant fox.

Begin stitching the fox by counting the aida square from the marked centre point and, starting at his chest, work in

beige (2013) and white, then work out and complete the rest of the fox using rust (2306) and pinky brown (2311), combining these two shades in the needle for parts of his fur if you wish. Stitch his legs in dark grey (1810) and pearl grey (1808), and the tip of his tail in beige and white. Work the grass around the fox in dull green (1602) and pale green (1401).

Next move to the right-hand side of the picture and stitch the tree in mid brown (2007) and tan (2008). Don't forget the grass at the base. The crow is in slate grey (1713) and black with a pearl grey beak. Add the cheese and the crow's beady eye in bright yellow (0114). Finally, fill in the trees, bushes, clouds and fence in the background.

When all the cross-stitching is complete, work the back-stitched lines using just one

"To the Hare's amazement he saw that he had lost the race." The hare in this picture is worked in various shades of brown with a white and cinnamon chest.

bright idea

These embroidered panels are just the right shape to make a book jacket for a hard-back book of a similar size or slightly larger – if it is a copy of Aesop's *Fables,* so much the better. You will need more fabric than that specified in the You Will Need box. Measure the book to see how much extra fabric is required around the design to fit the size of the book; you will also need to add 2cm at the top and bottom for a hem and 4cm at each end to form flaps into which to insert the book cover. If you do not want to use aida fabric all round the book, cut a piece of backing fabric instead and join this on at the spine.

strand of cotton in the needle. The fence is worked in dark grey and the grass is outlined in bottle green (1314). To complete this picture, stitch the border in dull pink (0809), teal blue (1712) and dark red (0407).

THE HARE AND THE TORTOISE

The hare in this story is so confident about winning the race which he is running with the tortoise that he dawdles on the way, never dreaming that the tortoise might catch him up. The tortoise plods methodically past him unnoticed and wins the race.

Begin stitching this picture by working the hare. The mottled effect on his chest is achieved by combining one strand of white and one strand of cinnamon (2011) in the needle. Complete the hare in taupe (1911), mid brown (2007), tan (2008), cinnamon and white with touches of slate grey (1713). Then fill in the grass and bushes around the hare in three shades of green with some dark red (0407) flowers on the left-hand bush. The tree is worked in mid brown and tan. Next work the path in pale grey (1709), adding the tortoise in the centre of it. When all the cross-stitching is finished, add the details on the

69

hare's feet with slate grey backstitch, using one strand of cotton. Complete the picture by stitching the border using the same colours as for The Fox and the Crow picture.

THE PEACOCK AND THE CRANE

In this fable, the peacock is boasting to the crane about its magnificently coloured feathers. "Your feathers may be more beautiful than mine," retorts the crane, "but I can fly and you cannot."

Begin stitching this picture with the peacock's tail. Work this in dark green (1404) and bottle green (1314) with dark blue (0913) and dull gold (2203) spots. The peacock's body is also stitched in these shades with an olive green (1608) edging; the beak is orange (1309). Work the shadow below the peacock in shades of blue and green with a touch of dull gold. Then add the crane flying over the peacock's head in white, pearl grey (1808) and dark grey (1810) with an orange crest. The clouds are light blue (0901).

When you have finished all the cross-stitching, outline the white parts of the crane in pearl grey backstitching, using one strand of cotton in the needle. Outline the peacock's body in dull gold in the same way. Using two strands

of orange, work the peacock's crest. Work the border as for The Fox and the Crow picture.

MAKING UP THE PICTURES

Press the pictures carefully from the wrong side over a lightly padded surface so as not to flatten the stitches. Check that you have not missed any stitches as these cannot be added once the designs are framed.

Place each picture face down on a table, put a piece of acid-free board centrally over the top and secure the fabric at the back with brown paper tape. Mount and frame.

"Your feathers may be more beautiful than mine," said the Crane, "but I notice that you cannot fly." The crane in The Peacock and the Crane picture is worked in white with grey and dark grey wing feathers and has a splash of orange on top of its head. The paler grey is also used to work a backstitch outline around the white areas to give them more definition.

STITCH DETAILS

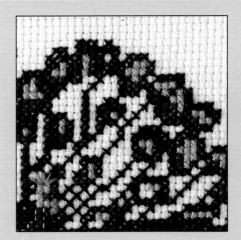

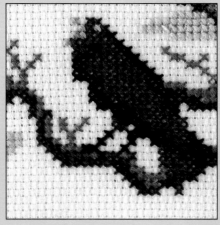

The peacock's feathers are worked in dark green, bottle green, dark blue and dull gold. A single strand of dull gold is also used to outline its body. Straight stitches in two strands of orange form the peacock's crest.

The crow sitting smugly in its tree is worked in slate grey and black with a pearl grey beak. His gleaming beady eye is worked in bright yellow. Add the branches of the tree in the shades of brown.

The victorious tortoise is seen overtaking the lazy hare in this picture. The road is worked in pale grey, while the tortoise is brown and green and has cinnamon and tan spots on the back of his shell.

Celestial clock

*Help a friend pass the time with this unusual needlepointed clock face
with traditional motifs of sun, moon and stars in a deep blue sky.*

Celestial clock

*T*he sun, moon and stars were often used to decorate antique clock faces to symbolise the passing hours, and this needlepoint version worked in half cross-stitch follows this tradition. The stylised sun at the centre surrounds the ornate hands. Roman numerals for twelve, three, six and nine are interspersed with small black dots to represent the remaining hours and add to the antique look. Although this clock has a delightfully old-fashioned look, at the back of the work is a modern, battery-operated quartz movement.

Bright shades of blue and yellow have been used to create a striking colour scheme. The face of the clock measures 15cm × 20cm.

STITCHING THE CLOCK

Fold the canvas lightly in half horizontally and vertically and mark the centre point. Mount the canvas in a slate frame if you wish to prevent it from distorting. Follow the chart shown opposite on which each square represents one half cross-stitch. The yarn colours are given in the key on the right.

Using two strands of yarn throughout, begin stitching from the centre outwards, leaving the small area at the very centre unworked where indicated to accommodate the spindle and hands of the clock movement. To secure the thread end, work the first few stitches over it at the back of the canvas; to finish off, pass the needle under the last few stitches at the back. Finish one area of colour before beginning the next.

The centre of the sun is worked in yellow (727) and the rays in dark gold (701) and mid gold (702). The dark background to the sun is worked in three tones of blue to give a shaded appearance. For certain stitches cut equal lengths of two different blues and mix them in the needle so that the colours blend into one another, referring to the chart on the opposite

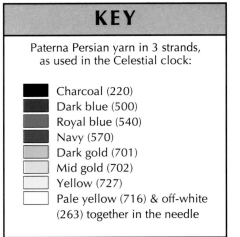
page and the colour key (above) for guidance.

When the inner area is complete, add the Roman numerals at the top, bottom and sides in charcoal (220). Work the hour and half-hour marks in charcoal and mid gold. Take care not to stretch the dark thread across the back of the canvas from one area of stitching to another as it may show through the pale stitching which you will be working next.

Now fill in the light-coloured background. For a slightly mottled, 'antique' effect, mix one strand of pale yellow (716) and one

A crescent moon and stars shine from a dark sky in the top panel of the clock.

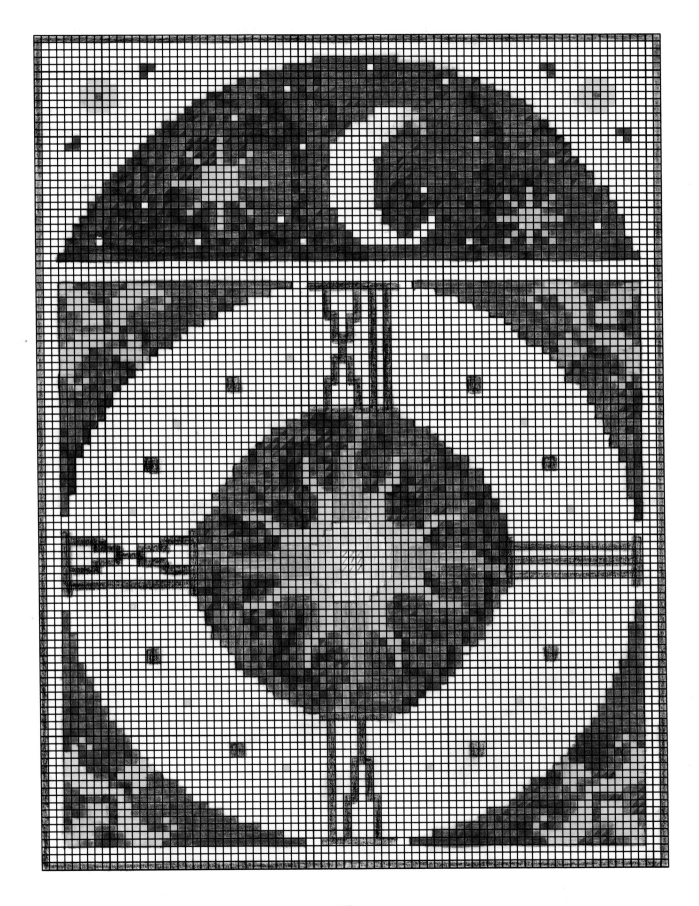

HOW TO FIT THE MOVEMENT

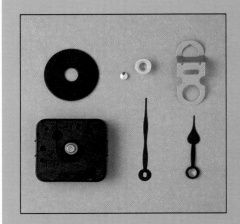

1 *The clock movement consists of a motor, rubber washer, two brass nuts, one hour hand, one minute hand and a hook.*

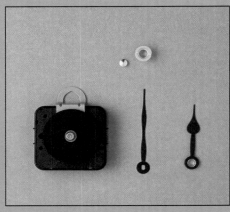

2 *First lay the hook over the front of the motor and then place the rubber washer on to protect the needlepoint.*

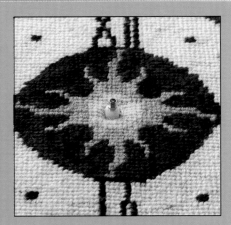

3 *Insert the central spindle of the mechanism up through the unstitched hole in the centre of the needlepoint.*

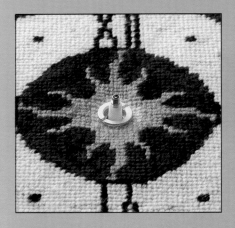

4 *Place the large brass nut over the spindle and carefully tighten it to hold the needlepoint and the movement together.*

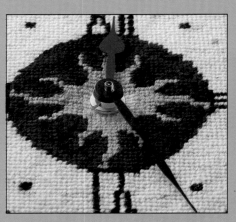

5 *Place the hour hand on the spindle, at the twelve o'clock position. Now fit the minute hand between the three and six o'clock position.*

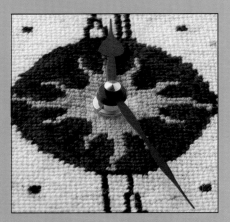

6 *To complete the installation, screw the small brass nut on to the end of the spindle to hold the hands in position.*

Each corner features a fleur-de-lis motif in mid gold yarn.

strand of off-white (263) in the needle and work with both together. Complete the main part of the face by working the fleur-de-lis motifs at the corners in mid gold and filling in the blue background.

Next work the moon and stars in the semi-circular celestial sky above the main area, adding scattered single stitches in off-white for the distant stars. Fill in the dark sky in the background as before. Finally work the circular motifs in the top corners and then fill in the light-coloured border with the pale yellow and the off-white yarns mixed. The completed design is outlined by a single-row border of half cross-stitches worked in charcoal yarn.

MAKING UP THE CLOCK
Take the needlepoint off the frame. Cut a hole in the unworked central area of the sun motif and fold the canvas under, securing the threads with small oversewing stitches. Place the clock face over a piece of stiff card or hardboard, cut slightly bigger than the worked area. Lace the raw edges of the canvas at the back of the card. Pierce or drill a 10mm hole in the card to match the central, unworked area of canvas. Attach the movement and the hands following the instructions given above. Frame the clock face as required.

Gold frame

This ornate frame, stitched in rich shades of yellow and gold,
makes an elegant decoration on any wall or dresser top.

Gold frame

Inspired by the gilded Venetian frames made in the Baroque style, this magnificent mirror frame imitates the splendour of a former age. An original frame would have been carved from wood and this technique has been recreated on canvas in a very simple way. In keeping with the original, the intricate edging of the frame has been shaped from plastic canvas and the effect of the gilded carving has been incorporated into the design. A wonderfully ornate look has been achieved using various shades of gold yarn and gold lurex thread.

CUTTING THE CANVAS

Despite the intricacy of the design, the frame is extremely easy to make. The overall shape is simply cut out from 10-gauge plastic canvas using the outline of the picture opposite. Transfer the pattern to the canvas and then, following the line, cut round the canvas using small, sharp scissors. The easiest way to transfer the pattern is to place the plastic canvas on top of the pattern sheet and then trace the outline on the canvas with a pencil – the pattern should be clearly visible through the holes of the canvas.

STARTING TO STITCH

When you have cut out the shape of the frame, it is a good idea to sort your yarns in good light and label them for easy colour reference. Making swatches before you start helps to avoid mistakes when stitching – particularly, as in this case, when the shades in the design are very similar. Now you are ready to start stitching the frame.

The mirror design, although beautifully ornate, is simply worked in cross-stitch using two strands of yarn throughout. Starting at the bottom of the frame, work in cross-stitch under the 'basket' using mid tan (700). Follow

YOU WILL NEED

- **32 × 24cm 10-gauge plastic canvas**
- **Paterna Persian yarn, two skeins each of:**
  Creamy yellow 715   411 Dark brown
  Mid tan 700
- **Three skeins of:**
  Golden yellow 702
- **Four skeins of:**
  Sunny yellow 726
- **One roll of lurex thread**
- **Tapestry needle**
- **15 × 20cm oblong mirror**
- **15 × 20cm card backing**
- **20 × 35cm backing fabric in a toning colour**
- **25 × 25cm felt**
- **6 × 18cm strong card**
- **Strong glue**
- **Sewing needle and thread**

the key and colour swatches as you stitch. When you are working over the outside edge of the frame, take the stitch around the outer edge of the canvas, making sure that all of the canvas is well covered by the yarn.

Fill in all the other tan areas in the design – these will provide the basis of the shading in the design to mirror the carved wood effect. Then using dark brown (411), stitch the shadow underneath the 'basket' and continue to work the other dark shading throughout the design in the same colour. Move on to work the two gold colours around these shaded areas, referring to the chart at every stage. Take care when using golden yellow (702) and sunny yellow (726) as it is easy to confuse the two shades – check your colour swatches when you are changing the yarn in your needle. Then add the pale highlights in the design using creamy yellow (715). Finish off the thread on the back of the work as neatly as you can and trim off any loose ends.

Finally the baroque-style frame is 'lifted' in a special way – a gilded effect is achieved using gold lurex thread dotted here and there throughout the design. Used sparingly, it imitates the sparkle of gold leaf which was used in carvings during the Middle Ages. Mix one long double length of lurex thread with sunny yellow and creamy yellow to highlight

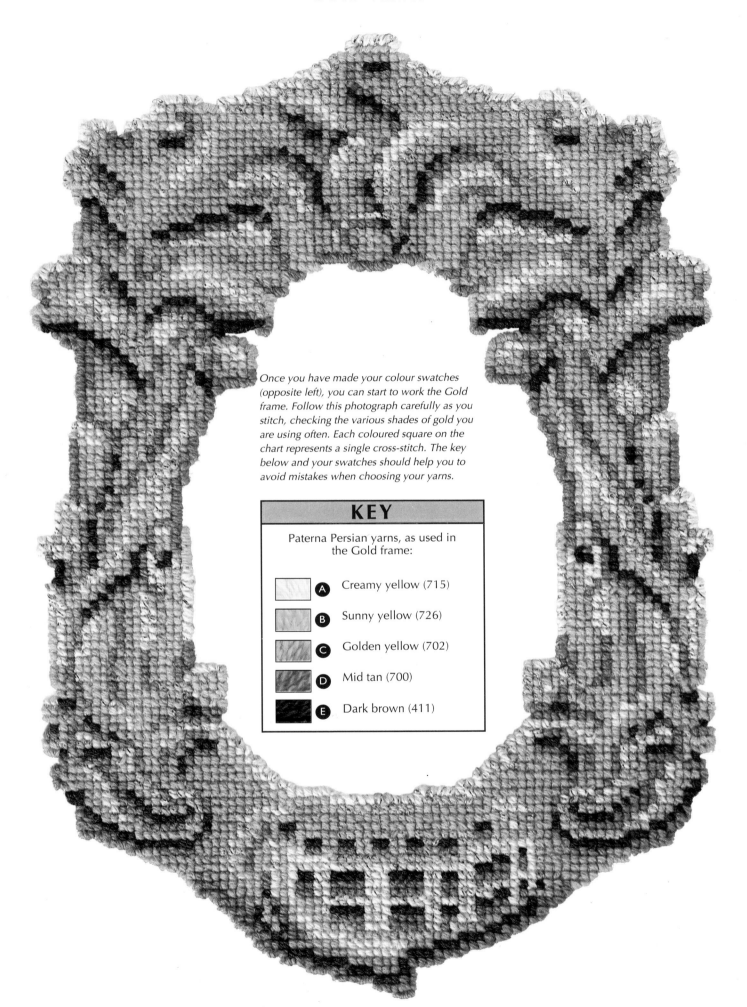

Once you have made your colour swatches (opposite left), you can start to work the Gold frame. Follow this photograph carefully as you stitch, checking the various shades of gold you are using often. Each coloured square on the chart represents a single cross-stitch. The key below and your swatches should help you to avoid mistakes when choosing your yarns.

KEY

Paterna Persian yarns, as used in the Gold frame:

- **A** Creamy yellow (715)
- **B** Sunny yellow (726)
- **C** Golden yellow (702)
- **D** Mid tan (700)
- **E** Dark brown (411)

bright ideas

If you would rather make a picture frame instead of a mirror frame, it is very simple to do. When you make the stitched canvas into a frame, as in the steps opposite, make a few minor adjustments and your photograph or picture frame will take shape. Instead of a mirror, you will need a piece of glass cut to the same measurements. Old picture frames can be found cheaply in markets and jumble sales and they sometimes have glass in useful sizes – otherwise, you will need to have glass cut to size. Insert the glass behind your frame in place of the mirror and present it to a lucky recipient.

the 'basket' and the scrolls. This is not necessary for every length of yarn you use in these colours, but it will give a glint to certain areas. Be careful not to get carried away – too much lurex thread in the design will make your frame look gaudy. When you have added the glistening highlights, your gold frame is ready to be made up.

MAKING UP THE FRAME

Before you make up the frame, you should assemble all the materials you need. You can buy a standard oblong mirror in most department stores. If not, a hardware store will cut a mirror to size for you.

Choose a medium-weight backing fabric in a colour which complements the design. The felt can be black as shown here or can be of a colour to match the backing fabric. The back of the mirror frame is very simply sewn together. Cut out your card backing to the size of the mirror and your backing fabric about 1.5cm larger all round.

To make the stand, cut a wedge-shaped piece of strong card 18cm long and 10cm wide at the thicker end and 4cm wide at the thin end. At the thin end of the stand, bend the card over about 4cm to make a hinge. Then cut out a covering for the stand from felt – use the card stand as a guide and cut it so that the felt will overlap a little on the back to cover the card completely. Now you are ready to make up the frame – see the steps opposite for details.

HOW TO MAKE THE FRAME

1 Place canvas face down on a flat work surface. Put mirror face down on top, then card backing and then backing fabric with the wrong side against the card.

2 Turning in a 0.5cm hem all round, pin fabric to back of stitched canvas so that it holds the mirror and the card in place. Make sure that the mirror sits square in the frame.

3 Oversew the edges in matching sewing thread. Use small, neat stitches, worked very close together so that all the layers are held secure. Remove the pins as you go.

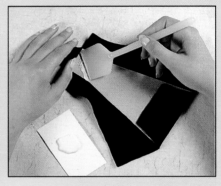

4 Cut out card mirror stand and felt cover as described in the main text. Lay card on felt and fold in fabric flaps at either end and stick them to the card using strong glue.

5 Once the glued felt ends are secure, glue down one side flap of felt, pressing it smooth over the card. Then fold in the remaining flap of felt and glue in place, tucking the corners in neatly.

6 Glue square top of stand above the bending hinge to back of mirror about 10cm down from frame top. Turn glued seams of stand inwards. Oversew round the stand top using matching sewing thread.

Old master

Bring some fine art into your home with this needlepoint picture based on a landscape painting by Gainsborough.

Old master

YOU WILL NEED

- **47 × 65cm 10-gauge single canvas**
- **Paterna Persian yarn, one skein each of:**

Teal blue 523	635 Spring green
Ginger 882	515 Old blue
Flesh 493	263 White
Mauve 314	505 Mid blue
Grey 203	494 Pale pink
Black 220	703 Bright yellow
Dark blue 501	

- **Two skeins each of:**

Pale gold 744	724 Golden yellow
Dark brown 450	453 Light brown
Copper 720	613 Light leaf green
Lovat green 663	422 Coffee
Pale grey 256	

- **Three skeins each of:**

Pale shamrock 622	612 Mid leaf green
Pine green 661	690 Dark olive green
Mid olive green 652	641 Khaki
Mid brown 412	D501 Sea green
Pale sea green D503	

- **Tapestry needle**

KEY

Paterna Persian yarn for the Old master:

523	501	622
882	744	612
515	724	661
493	450	690
263	453	652
314	720	641
505	613	412
203	663	D501
494	422	D503
220	256	635 +
703		622

*I*nspired by a landscape painting by Gainsborough, this peaceful rural scene is worked entirely in half cross-stitch. In the foreground and centre of the picture, some activity is provided by ducks swimming on a pond and a hay-cart being loaded by

farm workers, with their horse quietly grazing. A church and a cottage peep through the trees in the background. The sky, which is worked in mottled shades of blue and mauve, has light clouds floating across it.

In a beautiful antique-look frame, this picture would make a particularly charming gift, perhaps to a friend who has moved into a country cottage, but would also be appropriate in any period house with traditional furnishings. It measures 36cm by 55cm.

PREPARING THE CANVAS

Bind the raw edges of your canvas with masking tape to prevent the wool yarn from catching on the ends of the canvas threads. Mount

The haywain and farm workers form the focal point of this charming picture.

the canvas in a slate frame if you wish, as this will help to keep the needlepoint in shape as you work it (see page 18).

STITCHING THE SCENE

The chart for the country scene is shown on the previous two pages. Each square equals one half cross-stitch and the colours to use are indicated in the key. Before you begin stitching, mark the centre of the canvas horizontally and vertically with lines of tacking. Also mark the centre lines of the chart in pencil to correspond.

As so many shades of green are used in the picture, you will find it very helpful to sort the different-coloured yarns on to project cards, which are available from the haberdashery section of department stores or good craft and needlework shops. You can also make your own by cutting lengths of stiff card and punching holes along one long edge. Cut your yarn into working lengths of about 45cm and loop them through the holes. Then write the shade name and number beside each hole. It will then be

easier to find the correct colour as you reach it on the chart.

Begin stitching the picture centrally at the dark olive green tree, using two strands of yarn in the needle. To secure your thread end at the back, leave a short length and work the first few stitches over it; to finish off neatly, run the needle through the last few stitches worked at the back. Complete one area of colour before beginning the next. However, where there are a lot of small areas of colour, thread several needles with different colours so that you can use them as you come to each colour. Keep the ones not currently in use pinned in the canvas margin, well away from the stitching area. Remember not to take the yarn across the back of the canvas from one area to another, as it will get caught up in subsequent stitching and cause unsightly lumps on the front of the work.

When you have completed the dark-coloured tree in the centre of the picture, continue with the trees on the right of it. Then add the white cottage and the pale grey church behind the trees. Next work the trees on the left-hand side, continuing with the hay-cart, the two figures and the horse. Some of these areas are filled in with two shades of yarn (pale shamrock green 622 and spring green 635) used together in the needle as indicated on the chart. To complete the top half of the picture, fill in the sky in mid blue, grey and mauve with pale pink clouds.

Now work the foreground of the picture. The grass is worked with some areas requiring mixed strands of green as described for the trees above. The dark reflections in the pond are worked in shades of coffee, dark brown, mid brown and copper. Stitch the water in shades of blue, green and grey. The water plants and the ducks add detail to the pond.

FINISHING OFF

Remove the completed needlepoint from the frame, if you used one, and block the canvas if necessary (see page 115). Mount and frame the picture in an antique-effect frame.

Cornucopia posy

Alive with colourful summer blooms, this pretty sampler
will bring a breath of fresh air to any room.

Cornucopia posy

Worked in counted cross-stitch in delicate pastels, this cornucopia of fresh flowers is a delight to stitch and something to treasure. The design is bursting with colourful blooms and a sense of movement has been created by the use of delicate falling petals. The background is worked in a lattice effect and each corner of the sampler is decorated with a pretty blue bow.

WORKING THE DESIGN

Fold your fabric in half and in half again to find the centre and then mount it in an embroidery hoop. The chart photograph is on the page opposite – use the key to help you to identify the colours. Start at the centre of the design and work outwards. Thread your needle with bronze (2203) and start stitching the cornucopia itself in counted cross-stitch.

Secure the end of the thread on the back by working your first few stitches over the thread. Work all the bronze in the cornucopia and then fill in the pale blue (0908). Work in rows wherever possible for an even tension.

Next move up to work the flowers and the leaves. Start stitching the leaves at the top of the cornucopia using olive (1609) and pale green (1501). Then add the shading in green (1502) and the lighter areas in grass green

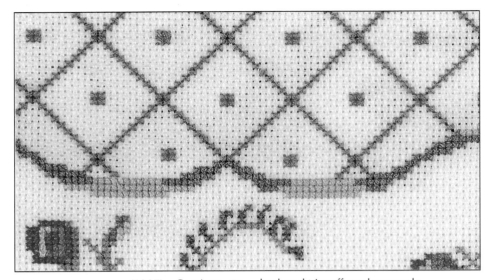

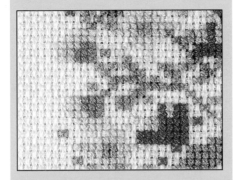

The purple flowers are worked in purple (0713) with highlights in lilac (0801). Yellow (0109) adds a bright touch to the design, forming daisy-like flowers and the petals of rose pink carnations (0610). Dots of mid blue (1012) soften the overall look.

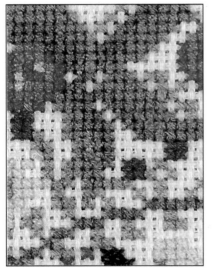

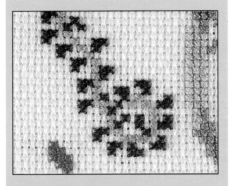

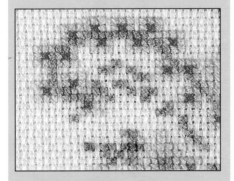

(1307). Continue to work in these shades of green throughout the bouquet, filling in all the stems and leaves. Follow the key carefully when threading your needle with similar shades of green.

When you have completed the leaves, you can work the flowers (see the Stitching details). Start with yellow (0109) and then add shading in orange (0114). Then stitch the violets in purple and lavender, the forget-me-nots in mid blue (1012) and the carnations in the three shades of pink. Fill in the falling petals using dark pink (0507) and yellow (0109).

Move outwards to work the blue ribbon border. Start in the middle at the top using mid blue. Then stitch in pale blue and continue, alternating the two colours. Do not be tempted to carry the thread too far across the back of the fabric as it might show through.

Next add a bow in each corner of the design working in both shades of blue. Count the holes of the fabric carefully so that the bows are positioned symmetrically in the design. Finish off the thread neatly on the

back and trim off any loose ends.

With the details complete, work the background trellis using pale green (1501). You should pay particular attention to this aspect of the design as it is very easy to count the holes of the fabric incorrectly and the trellis will then not be square to the design. Stitch the lines of the trellis in diagonal rows, keeping an even tension in your stitches. Your final step is to stitch four cross-stitches for the dots in each trellis square using rose (0610).

FRAMING

When the embroidery is complete, remove the fabric from the hoop or frame and trim off any loose thread ends on the back. Press lightly from the back with a warm, dry iron to remove the creases formed by the hoop and the sampler is ready to frame. You can buy a ready-made frame and mount from a specialist framer or have the frame cut to size. Choose a mount which complements the design. Stretch the sampler in the frame and present it to a lucky friend.

The twisting stems and leaves featured here are filled in using grass green (1307) and green (1502). These two shades create an attractive contrast. The falling petals are mainly worked in dark pink (0507). Those at the bottom of the cornucopia are yellow.

The stems of the yellow (0109) flowers are pale green (1501) and those of the forget-me-nots are grass green (1507). Dark pink (0507) forms the centre of the yellow flowers. The forget-me-nots are mid blue.

Guest towels

Use the charts and keys on this page to work the cross-stitch designs for the pair of guest towels on page 51.

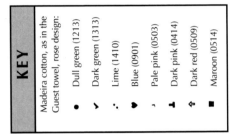

page 51.

KEY	
Madeira cotton, as in the Guest towel, rose design:	
●	Dull green (1213)
➤	Dark green (1313)
∴	Lime (1410)
◗	Blue (0901)
↵	Pale pink (0503)
◢	Dark pink (0414)
⬧	Dark red (0509)
■	Maroon (0514)

Each square on the chart represents one cross-stitch worked over one square of evenweave fabric. Before you start, follow the direction of the arrows to find the centre square so that you can position the design squarely on the fabric.

KEY	
Madeira cotton, as in the Guest towel, heart design:	
∴	Mint (1208)
●	Dull green (1213)
◗	Mid green (1303)
◖	Blue (0901)
↵	Pale pink (0503)
◢	Dark pink (0414)
E	Bright red (0210)

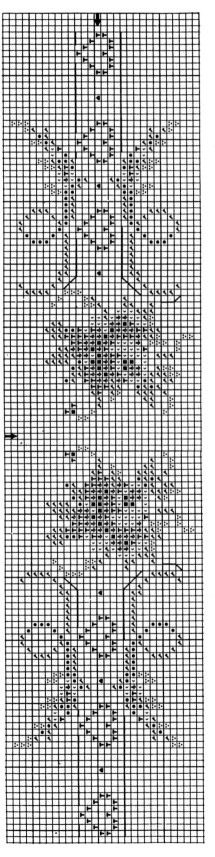

Victorian sampler

Use this chart and key (right and facing page) to work the cross-stitch design for the Victorian sampler on page 25. Each square on the chart represents one cross-stitch worked over one square of aida fabric. Take care when matching each section of the design either side of the 'overlap' line.

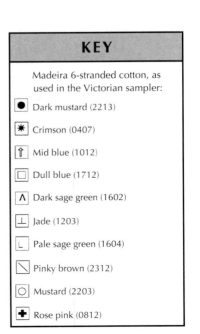

KEY

Madeira 6-stranded cotton, as used in the Victorian sampler:

● Dark mustard (2213)

✳ Crimson (0407)

⬆ Mid blue (1012)

☐ Dull blue (1712)

∧ Dark sage green (1602)

⊥ Jade (1203)

L Pale sage green (1604)

╲ Pinky brown (2312)

○ Mustard (2203)

✚ Rose pink (0812)

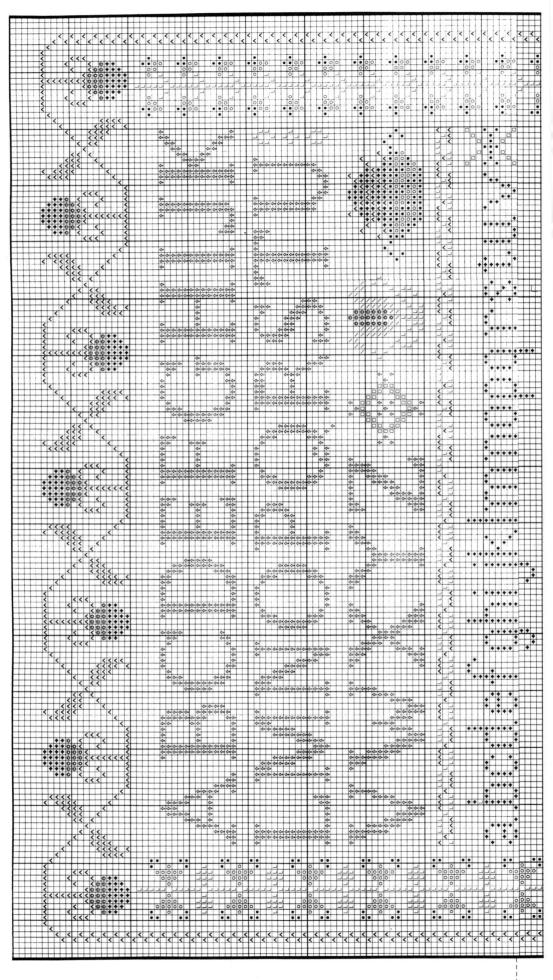

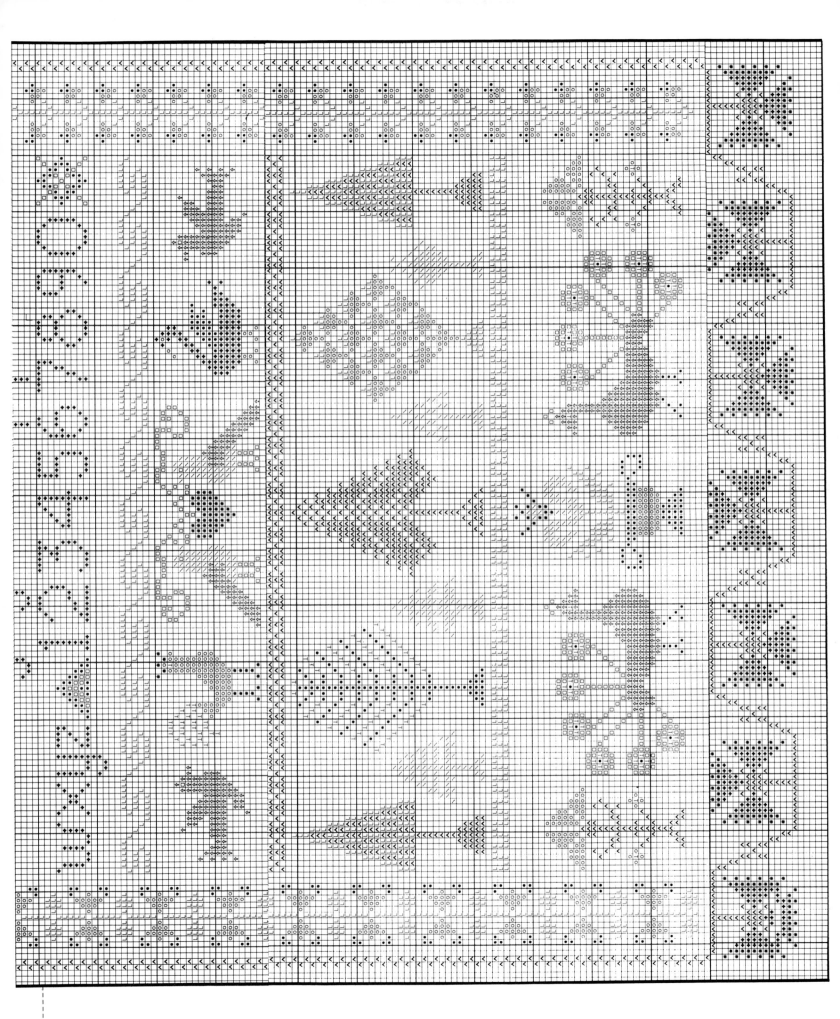

OVERLAP

Baby blanket

Use these charts and keys to work the cross-stitch design for the Baby blanket (page 59). The diagram (below, top left) will help you position the different elements of the design on the blanket. Each square on the charts represents one cross-stitch worked in Madeira cotton over one square of the evenweave fabric. Take care when matching each section of the central design either side of the 'overlap' line (below, bottom, and facing page). Stitch the heart border motif for the upper left hand corner (below, top right) as is, then repeat the border only, minus the heart, on either side. Repeat the whole design for each of the other three corners, turning the pattern so that the point of the heart always faces into the centre of the blanket.

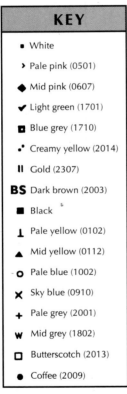

KEY	
•	White
➤	Pale pink (0501)
◆	Mid pink (0607)
✔	Light green (1701)
▣	Blue grey (1710)
∴	Creamy yellow (2014)
‖	Gold (2307)
BS	Dark brown (2003)
■	Black
⊥	Pale yellow (0102)
▲	Mid yellow (0112)
○	Pale blue (1002)
✕	Sky blue (0910)
+	Pale grey (2001)
w	Mid grey (1802)
▢	Butterscotch (2013)
●	Coffee (2009)

Sweet Dreams

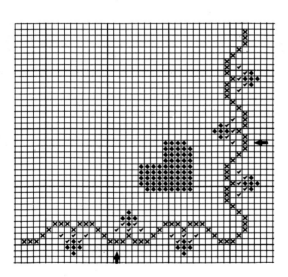

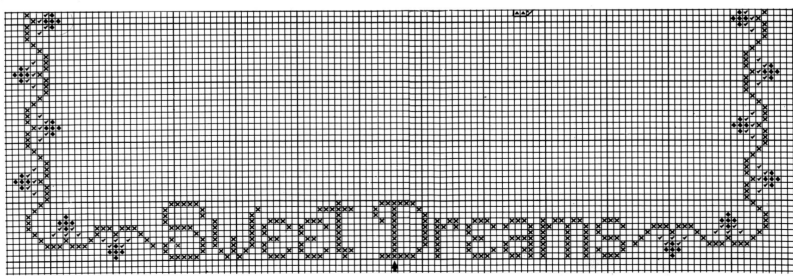

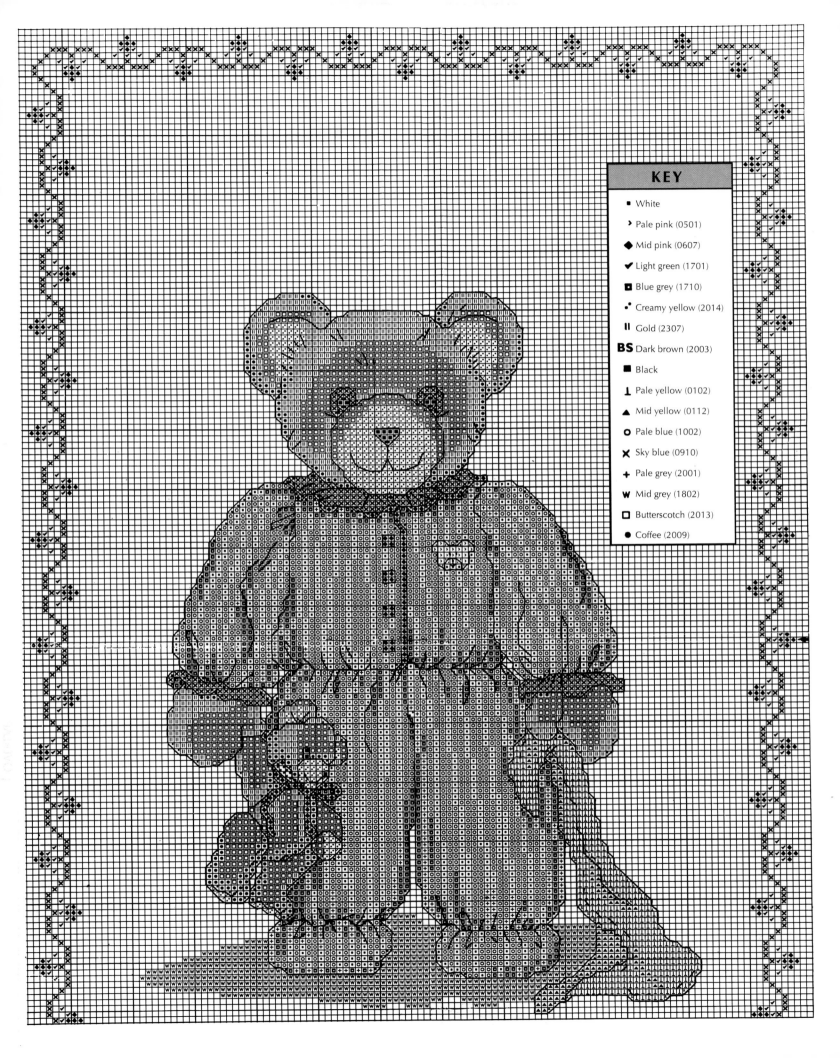

KEY

- ■ White
- ❯ Pale pink (0501)
- ◆ Mid pink (0607)
- ✔ Light green (1701)
- ▣ Blue grey (1710)
- • Creamy yellow (2014)
- ‖ Gold (2307)
- **BS** Dark brown (2003)
- ■ Black
- ⊥ Pale yellow (0102)
- ▲ Mid yellow (0112)
- O Pale blue (1002)
- ✕ Sky blue (0910)
- ＋ Pale grey (2001)
- W Mid grey (1802)
- ▢ Butterscotch (2013)
- ● Coffee (2009)

Aesop's fables pictures

Use the charts and combined key (right and facing page) to work the cross-stitch designs for the three Aesop's fables pictures on page 67: The Hare and the Tortoise (this page); The Fox and the Crow (page 93, left); The Peacock and the Crane (page 93, right). Each square on the charts represents one cross-stitch worked over one square of aida fabric.

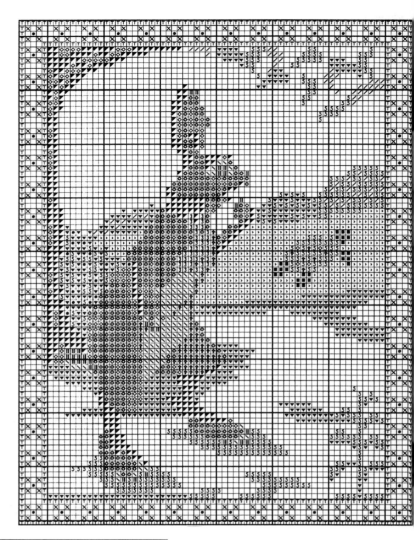

KEY

Madeira 6-stranded cotton, as used in
the Aesop's fables pictures:

△	Bright yellow (0114)	●	Dark red (0407)
⇩	Orange (0309)	◤	Mid brown (2007)
8	Light blue (0901)	◇	Tan (2008)
◥	Dark blue (0913)	V	Rust (2306)
✗	Teal blue (1712)	⊥	Pinky brown (2311)
>	Pale grey (1709)	⇧	Cinnamon (2011)
▣	Grey (1801)	Ⅰ	Dull gold (2203)
✓	Pearl grey (1808)	˙	Beige (2013)
L	Dark grey (1810)	✳	Taupe (1911)
Ⅱ	Slate grey (1713)	T	Dull pink (0809)
≡	Bottle green (1314)	■	Mid brown & dark
▼	Pale green (1401)		sea green (2007/1705)
·l	Dark green (1404)	3	White & cinnamon
⋀	Dull green (1602)		(white/2011)
5	Olive green (1608)	+	Black
╱	Dark sea green (1705)	╲	White

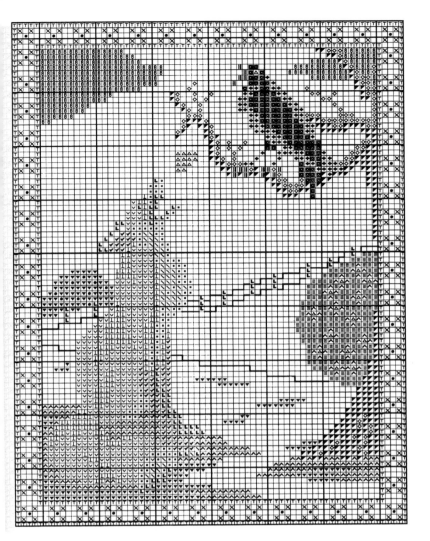
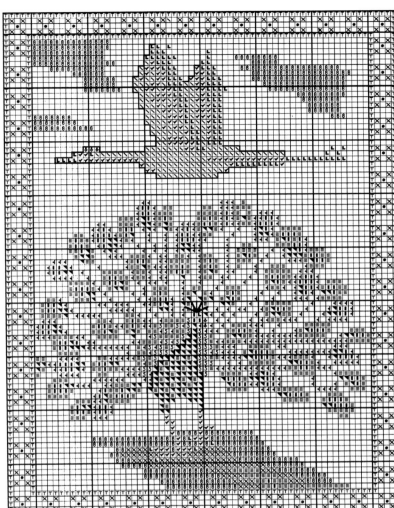

KEY

Madeira 6-stranded cotton, as used in
the Aesop's fables pictures:

△	Bright yellow (0114)		●	Dark red (0407)
↓	Orange (0309)		◤	Mid brown (2007)
8	Light blue (0901)		◇	Tan (2008)
◣	Dark blue (0913)		V	Rust (2306)
✕	Teal blue (1712)		⊥	Pinky brown (2311)
>	Pale grey (1709)		⇧	Cinnamon (2011)
▣	Grey (1801)		I	Dull gold (2203)
✓	Pearl grey (1808)		◦	Beige (2013)
L	Dark grey (1810)		✳	Taupe (1911)
Ⅱ	Slate grey (1713)		T	Dull pink (0809)
≡	Bottle green (1314)		■	Mid brown & dark
▼	Pale green (1401)			sea green (2007/1705)
⋅	Dark green (1404)		3	White & cinnamon
▲	Dull green (1602)			(white/2011)
5	Olive green (1608)		+	Black
╱	Dark sea green (1705)		╲	White

Nursery rhyme quilt

Use the charts and keys that follow to work the cross-stitch design for the Nursery rhyme quilt on page 63. Each square on the chart represents one cross-stitch worked over one square of aida fabric.

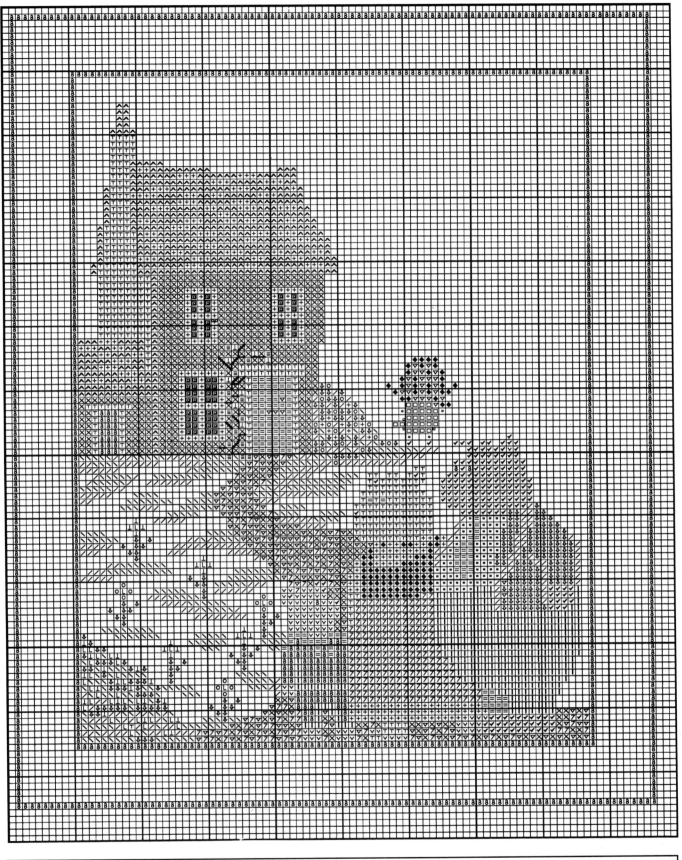

KEY							
◿ Light green (1310)	⟋ Jade green (1213)	☑ Pinky brown (2311)	▣ Dark red (0513)
◠ Dark flesh (0303)	☰ Dark green (1314)	⌃ Grey (1808)	⊤ Copper brown (2009)
↓ Lime green (1307)	▽ Gold (2211)	◆ Yellow (0108)	☰ Bright blue (0911)
✓ Dark brown (2007)	✕ Beige (2013)	▫ Flesh (0305)	⊥ Cyclamen pink (0708)
⌶ Pale pink (0502)	⏐ Slate blue (1712)	+ Violet (0903)	● Red (0210)
▣ Pale grey (1709)	O Purple (0713)	8 Pale blue (0907)	7 Pale yellow (0112)

KEY

◹ Light green (1310)	◿ Jade green (1213)	☑ Pinky brown (2311)	◻ Dark red (0513)
△ Dark flesh (0303)	☰ Dark green (1314)	⌃ Grey (1808)	⊤ Copper brown (2009)
↓ Lime green (1307)	▽ Gold (2211)	◆ Yellow (0108)	☰ Bright blue (0911)
☑ Dark brown (2007)	✕ Beige (2013)	⊡ Flesh (0305)	⊥ Cyclamen pink (0708)
⊔ Pale pink (0502)	Ⅰ Slate blue (1712)	⊞ Violet (0903)	● Red (0210)
▣ Pale grey (1709)	○ Purple (0713)	8 Pale blue (0907)	7 Pale yellow (0112)

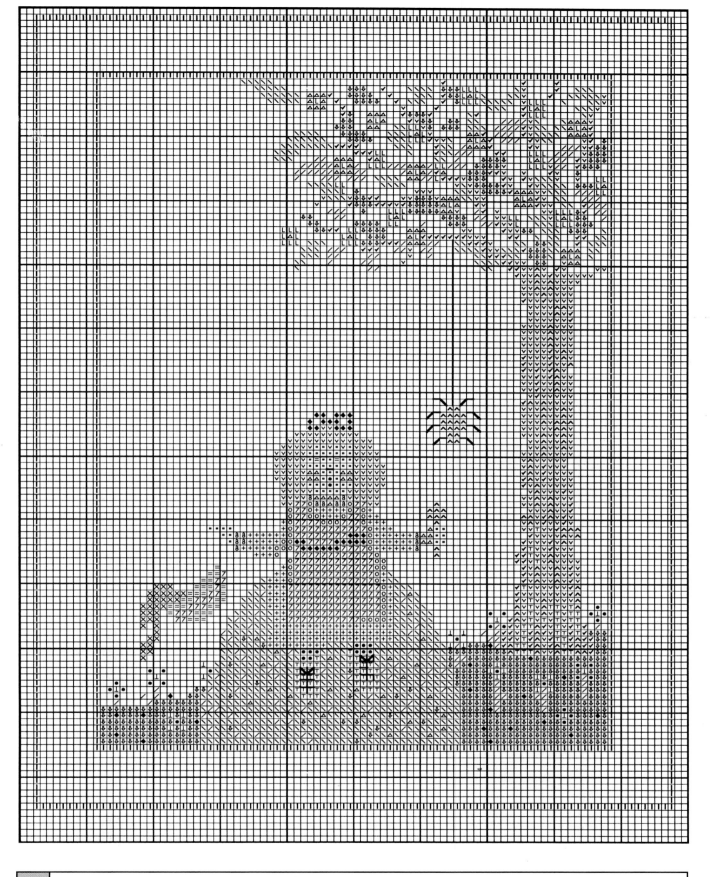

KEY						
⊠	Light green (1310)	⊡	Jade green (1213)	☑	Pinky brown (2311)	⊡ Dark red (0513)
△	Dark flesh (0303)	☰	Dark green (1314)	⌃	Grey (1808)	⊤ Copper brown (2009)
↓	Lime green (1307)	▽	Gold (2211)	◆	Yellow (0108)	⊟ Bright blue (0911)
✓	Dark brown (2007)	⊠	Beige (2013)	⊡	Flesh (0305)	⊥ Cyclamen pink (0708)
⊔	Pale pink (0502)	⊤	Slate blue (1712)	⊞	Violet (0903)	● Red (0210)
◉	Pale grey (1709)	○	Purple (0713)	8	Pale blue (0907)	7 Pale yellow (0112)

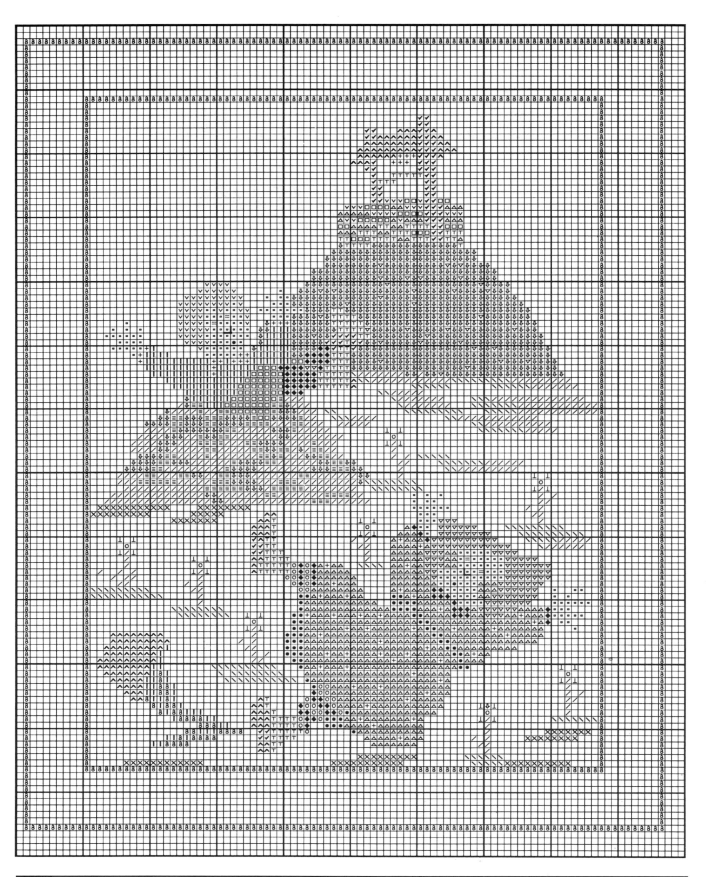

KEY							
◣	Light green (1310)	◪	Jade green (1213)	☑	Pinky brown (2311)	▣	Dark red (0513)
△	Dark flesh (0303)	⊟	Dark green (1314)	⌃	Grey (1808)	T	Copper brown (2009)
↓	Lime green (1307)	▽	Gold (2211)	◆	Yellow (0108)	=	Bright blue (0911)
✓	Dark brown (2007)	✕	Beige (2013)	⊡	Flesh (0305)	⊥	Cyclamen pink (0708)
⌐	Pale pink (0502)		Slate blue (1712)	+	Violet (0903)	●	Red (0210)
▣	Pale grey (1709)	O	Purple (0713)	8	Pale blue (0907)	7	Pale yellow (0112)

Stitches and techniques

Stitches and techniques

*A*lthough needlepoint and cross-stitch are both simple and straightforward, there are a few basics with which beginners and addicts alike need to be familiar. The following section outlines the fundamentals of both types of embroidery, as well as describing a few of the techniques that you might want to know about to help you complete the more intricate projects.

Both needles and threads, essential for any embroidery you might undertake, come in an array of sizes and types – and in the case of threads and yarns, a huge variety of colours – that can be confusing to the newcomer. We take you through this maze briefly, but you will probably find that you want to explore the field more thoroughly on your own by visiting needlecraft shops and fairs to see for yourself the incredible range of threads, yarns, fabrics and types of canvas available.

Some of the projects in *Gifts and Heirlooms* include stitches other than the traditional tent stitch and cross-stitch – in particular, the backstitch or Holbein stitch used to outline motifs worked in cross-stitch. Long stitch is a simple straight stitch that can be used horizontally or vertically very effectively.

The other section of this chapter provides information about making up and finishing your completed projects. The most beautifully stitched piece can be ruined by a poor finish, but all the techniques here are simple to do and will give a professional look to all your work. Making your own cushion pads, cords and braids is not only much less expensive than buying ready-made ones, it also means your finished item will be 'all of a piece' as you can use the same thread and fabric for finishing and match your colours exactly, and you can enjoy the satisfaction that goes with doing the whole job.

So don't worry about what to do with your completed work – just follow the clear step-by-step instructions in each section and you are on your way to creating a gift that will be treasured by the recipient, and could become a family heirloom.

Needles

Needles are, of course, essential items of sewing equipment.
Stock your workbox with a selection of different types,
so you'll always be sure to have just the right needle for each project.

For every stitching project, you need a needle – but what kind? There are so many different types and different sizes available that it's easy to become confused. Rest assured, however, as most of the rules for which needle you use for which type of embroidery are just common sense.

CHOOSING A NEEDLE

The size of your needle depends mainly on the size of your thread. The eye of the needle should be big enough to allow you to thread it easily, but small enough to hold the thread reasonably firmly once it is threaded. If the eye of your needle is too big, the thread will keep slipping out while you are sewing. The body of the needle should be just wide enough to draw the thread through your chosen fabric easily. If the needle is too fine, you will have to pull the thread through unnecessarily hard, which will affect the flow of your sewing and the tension of the stitches. If your needle is too large, you will make large holes in the fabric that will not be hidden by the thread once it is pulled through.

The type of needle you use also depends on the kind of embroidery that you are doing. The two categories of needle are those with sharp tips and those with rounded or blunt tips. Sharp-tipped needles are used for most kinds of surface embroidery on ordinary closely woven fabrics, and are available in several styles and many sizes to suit different threads and techniques.

Needles with rounded tips are generally known as tapestry needles, and are used for stitching on fabrics with noticeable holes, such as evenweave linen, aida fabric, binca cloth and different types of canvas such as those used most often for needlepoint projects. Needles used on these fabrics do not need to pierce a hole to draw the thread through – in fact, a sharp tip is usually a drawback because it can split the threads or catch on the fabric and spoil the look of the finished piece.

NEEDLE TYPES

Below are listed the most common types of needle you will come across when planning embroidery and craft projects.

Tapestry needles (A) have blunt tips; they are available in many sizes to suit every kind of evenweave fabric. They are the most suitable needles for use with needlepoint canvas.

Crewels (B) are the most frequently used embroidery needles; they are available in many sizes and have a large, long eye that is ideal for threads such as stranded cotton, *coton perlé* and soft cotton.

Sharps (C) are fine needles with small eyes, useful for ordinary sewing thread, flower thread and *coton à broder.* These are ideal for working hemming stitches and tacking stitches on fine cotton fabrics.

Betweens (D) are sharp needles which are slightly shorter than sharps and can be useful for fine quilting projects.

Quilting needles (E) come in many sizes; they are often long, so that you can take several stitches with them at one time.

Beading needles (F) are long and very fine so they will pass through the fine holes in small beads without breaking them.

Chenilles (G) are fairly large sharp needles that have an extra-large eye for use with thick threads and yarns.

Rug needles (H) are like extra-large tapestry needles, and are used for stitching rugs either on canvas or large-gauge binca.

Bodkins (I) are large, blunt needles which can be used for threading yarn and elastic through casings and ribbon through eyelets.

Blanket needles (J) are very strong semi-circular needles for upholstery projects.

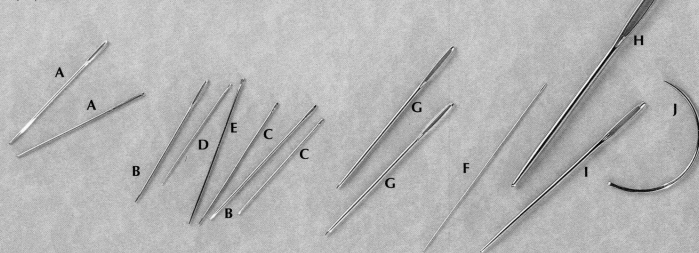

USING DIFFERENT NEEDLES

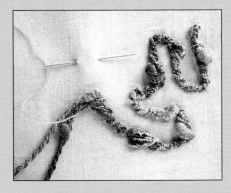

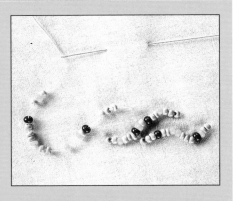

When you are embroidering in stranded cotton or a similar thread on closely woven fabric, a **crewel needle** is usually the best needle to use.

For single threads which you are using for embroidery stitches or for couching down thicker threads, choose a fine **sharps**, **between** or **crewel** needle.

Beading needles are especially long and fine so that they can pass through the tiny holes in small beads. For larger beads, use ordinary sharps and crewels.

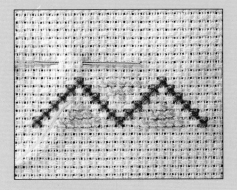

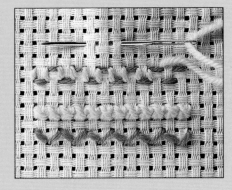

When you are working on fine evenweave fabric, such as linen, hardanger or aida fabric, use a fine or medium **tapestry needle** that will not split the threads as you stitch.

Larger-holed canvas needs to be worked with thicker threads and yarns to cover the background, so you will need a large-eyed **tapestry needle**.

If you are working on binca fabric or rug canvas which has very large holes, use a large tapestry needle or a special large-eyed **rug needle** which will be easy to thread.

WHAT WENT WRONG?

If the appearance of your embroidery does not seem quite right, you may discover that you have been using the wrong needle for the task.

In the first example, a crewel needle has been used instead of a blunt tapestry needle. The sharp tip has split the threads of the aida, producing uneven and unattractive cross-stitches.

In the second example, the needle is much too large for the background fabric, and has a blunt tip instead of a sharp one. It has made large holes in the fabric and the thread is too fine to fill and cover them.

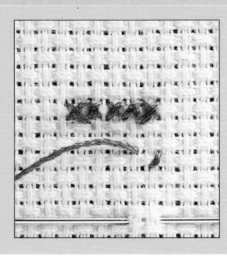

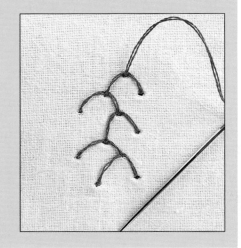

Threads

Any kind of thread can be used in embroidery, even ribbons, string or strips of leather, but cotton, wool and silk form the base for nearly all classic stitching styles.

Your choice of thread is affected by many factors, both practical and artistic. Some embroidery or needlepoint stitches require a particular thread or yarn, and you should always try to use a thread which can be worked easily on your ground fabric.

In general, threads can be divided into two types: stranded and twisted. Twisted threads are made up of plies, which cannot be pulled apart, but stranded threads can be easily separated and recombined to give the thickness of thread you need. A ply is a single thread of spun yarn and, generally, the more plies, the thicker the yarn. Each of the three strands of wool that make up the Persian yarn used in this book, for example, consists of two plies which cannot be separated.

Clockwise from top right: fine silk in colour-toned skeins, thick twisted silk, coton à broder, variegated cotton and pearl cotton; two wool yarns in stranded and twisted forms, matt embroidery cotton and metallic threads.

COTTON

Different weights and types of cotton are suitable for surface embroidery and counted, drawn and pulled-thread work. In six-stranded cotton the strands are easily divided for fine work – or it can be used as it is.

Soft embroidery cotton is a matt, medium-weight (5-ply), twisted thread, suitable for use on heavier fabrics, while pearl cotton (also called *perlé*) is somewhat finer. This 2-ply thread has a lustrous finish and is used in embroidery and also for smocking. It is

available in four different thicknesses: 3 (heavy), 5 (medium), 8 (fine) and 12 (very fine). *Coton à broder* is a twisted thread, finer than *perlé*, but with similar uses. All three can be effective when used on needlepoint canvas.

WOOL

Crewel wool is a 2-ply yarn in which the single strand is slightly finer than one strand of Persian wool. Unlike knitting yarns, crewel wool does not fray easily when pulled through fabric, so it is used in embroidery on heavy plainweave and evenweave fabrics in crewel work, and several strands thick for needlepoint.

Persian yarn is made up of three 2-ply strands and is the best choice for needlepoint on canvas, because you can vary the thickness to suit the gauge of the canvas. The same is not true of tapestry wool, a thick 4-ply wool, which is slightly finer than three strands of Persian yarn.

OTHER THREADS

Use silk thread for fine work on fine fabric. Available in stranded and twisted forms, it gives a lovely finish, and the results more than justify the cost. Similarly, linen is sold as matt thread for smocking and counted thread work, and in its shiny form for cutwork and drawn thread work. Synthetic metallic threads are available in various weights, textures and colours. They are ideal for highlighting or for small areas of solid stitching.

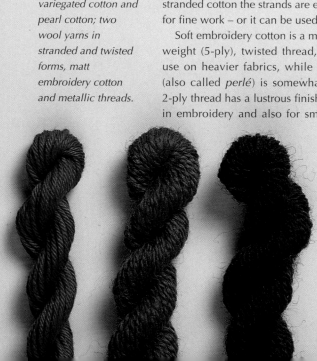

DIFFERENT EFFECTS WITH THREADS

Embroidery cotton – sold as coton à broder – a twisted cotton available in different plies, suitable for delicate embroidery on fine fabrics. As it is so fine, it is unsuitable for work on canvas or looseweave fabrics.

Matt embroidery cotton – a soft 5-ply twisted thread, ideal for work on medium- to loose-weave fabrics. Its thickness gives it good covering properties, making it suitable for fine needlepoint work too.

Perlé cotton – a thick, twisted 2-ply cotton, this pearly thread gives an attractive finish with a slight sheen. Suitable for use on medium- to loose-weave fabric and on fine needlepoint canvas.

Variegated cotton – a 2-ply pearlised cotton, thinner than regular perlé, with subtle repeating changes of shade down the length of the thread. The shading produces delicate effects in finished embroidery.

Crewel wool – a twisted yarn that is suitable in its single form for use on medium- to loose-weave fabrics, or for needlepoint on canvas in several thicknesses, depending on the gauge of the canvas.

Silk – a fine twisted 2-ply silk thread suitable for the finest embroidery on delicate fabrics. As it is so fine, it is sometimes easier to work with this silk using several thicknesses for better cover, as above.

Embroidery silk – this six-stranded thread can be used in any thickness to create satin-like effects. Although dearer than embroidery cotton, for special projects the results are well worth the extra cost.

Metallic thread – available in various thicknesses and with different degrees of metallic content, these threads can be used alone or, in the case of very fine metallics, mixed with plain threads to give highlights.

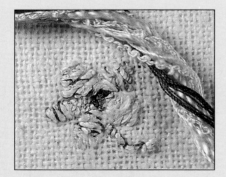

Mixed silks – sold in hanks consisting of a bouclé thread, a thick, soft thread, and strands of fine plain and variegated silk in toning colours, these blends are effective when used on loose weaves and knits.

Counted cross-stitch

Probably the oldest embroidery stitch of all, and certainly one of the quickest and easiest, counted cross-stitch is worked all over the world, in countries as far removed from each other as Mexico and India.

Cross-stitch has many uses. It can be worked as an outline or border, or as a filling stitch, and lends itself particularly well to lettering and motifs. Worked on canvas, it is very hard-wearing and so makes a good choice for upholstery.

Counted cross-stitch is usually stitched on special evenweave fabrics, such as aida, hardanger, linda or binca, or on canvas, because these make it easier to count threads, and the whole effect of the stitch depends on its regularity. Each cross-stitch should make a perfect square, being worked down and across over an equal number of threads.

Designs for counted cross-stitch are always presented in chart form, where one cross or symbol or block of colour denotes a single stitch. Using these charts is easy – you literally count your way across the design.

There are several ways of working basic cross-stitch. Choose your method according to the fabric or canvas you will be working on. When working cross-stitch on canvas, or making only the odd cross-stitch here and there, it is best to complete each cross before moving on to the next one.

If you are working cross-stitch in rows on an evenweave material, first work a line of diagonals in one direction, then cover them with 'top' diagonals, working in the opposite direction. By doing this you get a more even tension and finish. A variation of this, called alternate cross-stitch, involves working every other diagonal from right to left, then filling in the gaps by working another row of diagonals in the same direction before working the top diagonals in the same way. This ensures an even more regular tension and so is a particularly good choice if you want to fill a very large area with cross-stitch.

One rule applies to all methods: the top diagonal stitches must always lie in the same direction. If they do not, they will reflect the light differently from the other stitches and will stand out clearly as mistakes. The only exception is when you actually want to produce an uneven or irregular effect.

OUTLINE STITCH

Use Holbein stitch (also known as double running stitch) in combination with cross-stitch to outline and emphasise solidly stitched shapes and also to work decorative linear details. Holbein stitch worked as an outline is most successful when sewn on an evenweave fabric so that fabric threads can be counted to ensure perfect regularity.

Holbein stitch looks exactly the same on both sides of the fabric. It can be worked in straight lines or stepped to make a zigzag line when outlining a diagonal row of cross-stitches. The finished result looks rather like a row of backstitches, at least on the front. All the stitches should be of identical length.

Cross-stitch motifs can be as varied and colourful as you wish. From floral designs and alphabets to geometric borders, plain or fancy, you can create some lovely effects. Don't stick to printed charts either – have a go at designing your very own motifs and borders. Take your inspirations from some of the stitched examples that appear here.

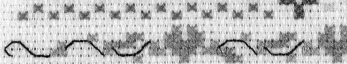

HOW TO WORK A SINGLE CROSS-STITCH

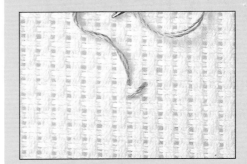

1 Make a diagonal stitch to the lower left, take the needle through to the back of the fabric and bring the needle back up at what will be the top left-hand corner of the cross.

2 Take the thread across the existing diagonal and insert the needle in the bottom right-hand corner of the cross, counting fabric threads to ensure each cross is worked over a square.

Various evenweave cotton and linen fabrics are specially produced for use with counted cross-stitch. The best-known is an evenweave cotton called aida. Three of the samples below are worked on aida; the 22-count fabric is cotton hardanger. Each sample has a different 'count', which has been worked on the front in cross-stitch. The count refers to the number of holes in the fabric (those large enough to pass a needle and thread through) per inch. The holes are all the same number of threads apart.

As shown below, the count of your background fabric affects the size of each cross-stitch, and thus the scale and size of your finished design, quite considerably.

HOW TO WORK CROSS-STITCH IN ROWS

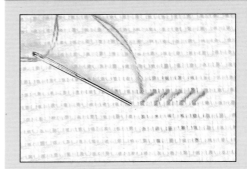

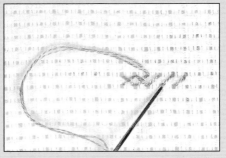

1 Make a diagonal stitch from top right to lower left. Bring needle out through the hole next to the start of the first stitch, ready to form the next, and continue.

2 At the end of the row, change direction and complete the crosses by working another row, this time working each diagonal from upper left to lower right.

HOW TO WORK HOLBEIN STITCH AS AN OUTLINE

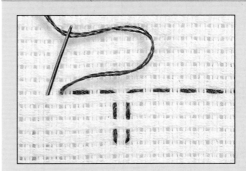

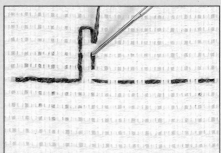

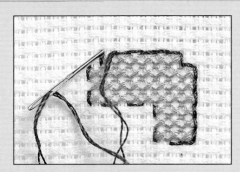

1 Work running stitches from right to left, following the outline of the shape. Each stitch should cover the same number of threads and the spaces in between should be the same size.

2 At the end of the row, turn the work round and work back over the row just done, filling in the spaces with another row of running stitch. Keep the tension even at all times.

3 Outline a row of diagonal cross-stitch by alternately working horizontal and vertical running stitches. The Holbein stitch should outline the shape with a narrow, continuous line.

Straight stitches

Simple to work and versatile, straight stitches are mainly used for working outlines and details. Variations of basic running stitch and backstitch can be used to decorate and enhance cross-stitch projects.

The basic straight stitches are running stitch, backstitch and stem stitch. They are all easy to work and can be used in a variety of situations on both plainweave and evenweave fabrics. They all form lines – useful for outlining shapes, working geometric designs and embroidering curved stems, as well as working intricate linear details. They can also be stitched in multiple rows to fill a shape; stem stitch is especially effective worked like this.

RUNNING STITCH

Although running stitch is the most basic of all embroidery stitches, it should not be ignored, as it can form exciting patterns when used imaginatively and, like many other simple stitches, it is often used as the basis of more elaborate techniques. Running stitch is also frequently used in quilting and appliqué. Double running stitch, generally known as Holbein stitch (see page 106), is worked twice over the same line, so that no spaces remain between the stitches. It makes a good outline worked in one or two colours and looks particularly effective on evenweave fabrics.

BACKSTITCH

Backstitch looks rather like Holbein stitch, but it produces a slightly raised line on the front of the fabric and is made up of longer overlapping stitches on the back. It has the appearance and something of the firmness of

machine stitching, and so is often used for closing seams when making up finished articles such as cushions.

As well as being used alone, running stitch, Holbein stitch and backstitch can form the foundation row for more complex stitches. In one of the most common variations, a second thread is woven in and out of the individual straight stitches to produce a whipped effect. When working a stitch like this, you will find it easier to use a blunt-pointed tapestry needle for the second thread. This will help you work the whipping row without picking up threads of the ground fabric.

All the stitches benefit from being worked perfectly regularly, unless your design actually requires a random effect. The weight of line each stitch produces can be varied by altering the size of individual stitches and by changing the weight and type of embroidery thread.

STEM STITCH

Stem stitch is a favourite choice for working stems, leaves and tendrils in floral designs. You make this stitch by working a series of sloping, overlapping straight stitches along a guideline marked on the fabric. You can vary the effect produced by the simple means of changing the angle of each stitch worked, to produce a narrower or broader line. Stem stitch also makes an effective border around pictures, cards and cushions worked in cross-stitch.

Practise the basic straight stitches together with some variations and create a beautiful border into the bargain by copying the border shown below. The stitches, from the outside in, are as follows: running stitch, double running (Holbein) stitch, whipped running stitch, backstitch, running stitch again, threaded backstitch and stem stitch. The paisley motif in the corner includes stem stitch and threaded backstitch.

HOW TO WORK RUNNING STITCH

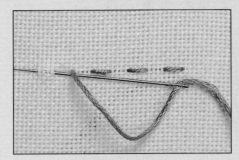

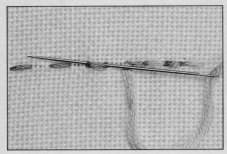

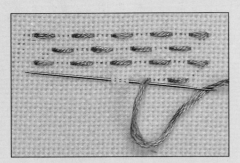

Simple running stitch is worked from right to left. Pass the needle through the fabric with an in-and-out movement. Keep the stitches the same length and the same distance apart.

To work *double running stitch*, also known as Holbein stitch, first sew a row of running stitches, then work a second row of running stitches to cover the spaces left on the first row.

Rows of *running stitch* make an effective border. Work a row of running stitches, then stagger the second row with stitches under the spaces in the row above. Repeat both rows.

HOW TO WORK BACKSTITCH

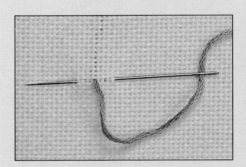

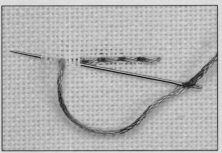

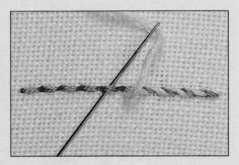

1 Pull thread through to fabric front and insert needle several fabric threads behind it. Bring point up same number of fabric threads in front of where sewing thread emerges.

2 Pull needle through in one motion, or make each stitch in two stages if fabric is stretched on a hoop. Repeat same sequence for each stitch. All stitches should be same length.

To work *whipped backstitch*, sew a row of backstitch, then cover with a row of whipping stitches as shown, taking the needle under each backstitch, not through the fabric.

HOW TO WORK STEM STITCH

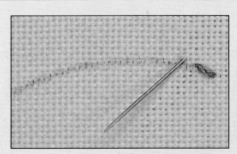

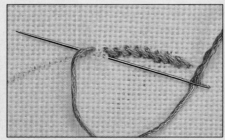

1 Stem stitch is similar to backstitch, except each stitch is at an angle to the guideline on the fabric. First, bring the thread through from the fabric back just above the guideline.

2 To make a stitch, insert the needle a little to the right, just below the guideline. Bring the point out to the left, just above the guideline, and pull the needle through in one motion.

To work *stem stitch as a filling*, work multiple rows, following the outline of the shape. Vary the position of the stitches on each row by making the first stitch slightly longer or shorter.

Continental tent stitch

Easy to learn and quick to do, tent stitch is a frequently used needlepoint stitch. It is also one of the most hard-wearing, which makes it particularly useful for cushions and upholstery.

Tent stitch, also known as 'petit point', is perhaps the most useful needlepoint stitch you will ever learn. A small diagonal stitch, tent stitch gives a smooth, flat surface which is ideal for creating pictures in wool from canvas, or forming a smooth background for other heavier, more textured needlepoint stitches.

SUPER STITCH

Continental tent stitch is the most versatile form of tent stitch. It can be worked in horizontal or vertical rows, or diagonally across the canvas. You will find it a particularly useful stitch for portraying intricate detail on canvas, or outlining a motif.

When working this form of tent stitch, there is a danger that the canvas will become pulled out of shape. To counteract this, try to maintain an even tension at all times. To guard against stretching the canvas out of shape, it is advisable always to work on a slate frame (see page 18).

A GOOD BEGINNING

If you have never worked tent stitch, practise on a scrap of canvas before embarking on a project. Use single canvas and a loosely twisted wool. Thread your needle with enough strands of yarn to cover the canvas adequately, but not so many that it will be difficult to pull the yarn through the holes, as this will produce a bulky, untidy effect.

Do not use too long a thread when stitching, as it will wear and break with the friction of being pulled through the canvas; 50cm is a good length. The thread will twist during stitching, so let the needle hang loose every so often. Work your way methodically across the canvas as far as possible, rather than darting about, doing a few stitches here and there. The back of your work should be almost as neat as the front! Avoid straggly ends by clipping off all secured threads as you go.

GUIDE TO CANVAS

Needlepoint canvas can be made of linen, plastic, paper, even silk, but the most popular material is cotton. Single canvas is made up of single vertical and horizontal threads. Double canvas is formed by the interweaving of parallel pairs of threads. Choose double canvas if your design is a complex one and is likely to include both large and small stitches.

There are two types of single and double canvas: evenweave, also known as plain, and interlock. The threads of evenweave canvas are not joined to each other, whereas the threads of interlock canvas are fused together at the points where they intersect. Evenweave canvas is best for upholstery and cushions because the threads are less likely to snap. Interlock canvas, however, does not become as distorted as evenweave canvas.

CONTINENTAL TENT STITCH

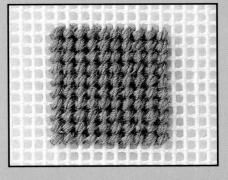

FRONT   The smooth texture of tent stitch as shown here can only be produced if the tension is even and the yarn is not pulled too tightly or allowed to be too slack.

BACK   When you are working continental tent stitch, the back of your canvas should be covered by long diagonal stitches, each one crossing two vertical canvas threads.

HOW TO WORK CONTINENTAL TENT STITCH

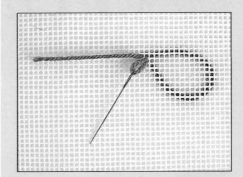

1 *(Back of work) Start by taking the needle through to the canvas front, passing it across one intersection and bringing it out again, leaving a yarn end of 4–5cm.*

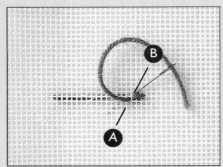

2 *To work a stitch, bring the needle out at A, take it over one intersection, insert it at B, pass it under two vertical threads and bring it out through the hole next to A.*

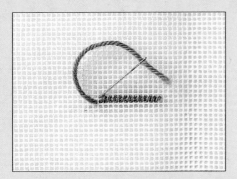

3 *Work in this way from right to left across the canvas. Use a stabbing motion, taking the needle right through to the canvas back before returning to the front again.*

4 *(Back of work) As you work, hold the yarn end against the canvas, so the first few stitches bind it in place. Trim off the remaining loose end and continue stitching.*

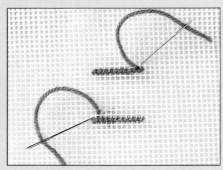

5 *Working from right to left, start a new row as shown (top) and continue. To start a new row working from left to right, move upwards as shown (bottom).*

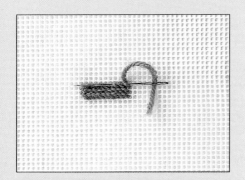

6 *(Back of work) To finish, weave the yarn through a few stitches, then snip off the end. Never knot yarn ends. Where possible, start new lengths of yarn in the same way.*

CONTINENTAL TENT STITCH WORKED VERTICALLY AND DIAGONALLY

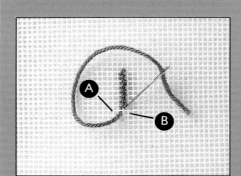

VERTICAL *To work a stitch in a vertical line, bring the yarn up at A, insert the needle at B, take the yarn under two horizontal threads and bring it up again one hole below A, ready to begin the next stitch.*

LEFT DIAGONAL *When you work a diagonal row down to the left, the stitches form a straight line – ideal for outlining. To form each stitch, take the needle diagonally under two vertical thread intersections.*

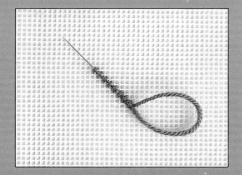

RIGHT DIAGONAL *A diagonal row down to the right produces a saw-toothed edge – the stitches do not touch. They can be visually linked by a line of yarn threaded under the completed row of stitches.*

Basketweave tent stitch

Popular with needleworkers since the earliest beginnings of needlepoint, this tent stitch variation remains one of the most versatile and durable of all canvaswork stitches. Use it for all types of upholstery for a really hard-wearing result.

Like the continental variety, basketweave tent stitch is a small, diagonal stitch which is worked on canvas. Both types of tent stitch are worked in rows, but the difference between the two is that continental tent stitch is worked horizontally or vertically and basketweave is worked diagonally. Although the two types of tent stitch look identical on the front of the work, the effect on the back of the canvas is very different. Basketweave tent stitch produces a distinctive interlocking or 'basketweave' effect – hence its name. The two stitches use about the same amount of wool but basketweave covers both sides of the canvas and produces therefore a very durable result. Most of the early needlepoint pieces which have survived through the centuries were worked in basketweave tent stitch, which shows how hard-wearing it is.

READING THE CANVAS

When working basketweave tent stitch on evenweave canvas, it is important to read the grain of the canvas for the best results. If you look closely at the canvas, you will see that at one intersection the vertical thread is on top and at the next the horizontal thread is on top. On a diagonal line of intersections, the top threads will all be either vertical or horizontal, alternating on each diagonal. The simple rule is: work rows down over vertical top threads and rows up over horizontal top threads.

Apart from producing a really smooth result, there are several advantages to reading the grain of the canvas. When you are working on very fine canvas,

you will prevent the stitches from disappearing between the threads of the canvas when they are worked in the wrong direction. Also you can work in different areas of the canvas and when you fill in the background, you will not get unsightly diagonal ridges where two adjacent rows are worked in the same direction. With some practice, you will soon be able to tell whether the next row to be worked should go up or down when you pick up a partially worked piece of canvas.

STITCHING IN ROWS

If you have never worked basketweave tent stitch before, it is best to practise on a piece of scrap canvas first before embarking on a needlepoint project. The short rows and the constant changing of direction can be confusing to a beginner and it is easy to miss stitches at the ends of the rows. Be careful not to make a half cross-stitch at the edges instead of a tent stitch – half cross-stitch covers the back of the canvas with very little wool and is less hard-wearing. If you find changing direction difficult at the end of each row, remember to rotate the needle one hole towards the centre of the design before you continue.

Basketweave tent stitch works best when used to fill in backgrounds or large areas of colour, as it does not distort the canvas and wears extremely well.

111

HOW TO WORK BASKETWEAVE TENT STITCH

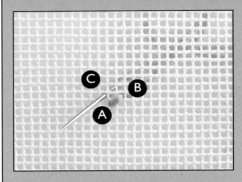

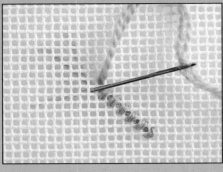

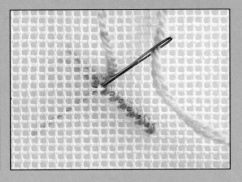

1 *Working diagonally, bring the needle out at A, take it up to the right over one intersection and insert it at B. Take the needle across two vertical threads and bring it out at C.*

2 *Continue working stitches up to the left in a diagonal line up to the end of the row. Work stitches over loose yarn at back of work while holding it in place with your finger.*

3 *To start the next row, take needle up across two vertical threads at the back and bring it out ready to form the next stitch. Continue as before, filling spaces left from previous row.*

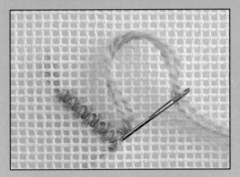

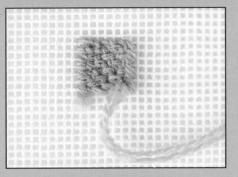

4 *To begin a third row, change direction by taking the needle up one horizontal thread and across two vertical threads at the back. Work in a diagonal row up to the left.*

5 *At the end of the third row, change direction as in step 3 to go diagonally down to the right again. Keep the edge of each new row in line with previously worked rows.*

6 *(Back of work) Secure the end of the yarn by passing the needle under a few stitches on the back. The rows of worked stitches form a distinctive basketweave pattern.*

BASKETWEAVE TENT STITCH AS A FILLING STITCH

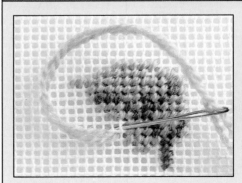

Work diagonally wherever possible to fill in areas of solid background colour. Once you have stitched the details of a design horizontally in continental tent stitch, fill in around the shapes using basketweave tent stitch.

Work basketweave tent stitch diagonally and continue in rows as explained in the steps above. This is the quickest and simplest way to fill in large areas of canvas. On the front of the work, the two types of stitches look identical.

On the back of the work, the difference between the rows of continental tent stitch (green) and the basketweave pattern (pink) is clear. Although worked differently, the two varieties use about the same amount of yarn.

Long stitch

One of the simplest of all needlepoint stitches, long stitch can be used to create textures, patterns and shading – and it is remarkably quick to cover canvas too.

The special feature of long stitch is that it is worked vertically or horizontally, but the stitches never cross the canvas threads diagonally – and you do not have to stitch into every hole, as with tent stitch. This makes it a very speedy stitch to work in, covering large areas quickly.

USING LONG STITCH

This quick 'filling' quality makes long stitch very popular for creating needlepoint pictures – its versatile length makes it ideal for subtle shading or texturing within a single colour area. Long stitch lends itself very well to geometric patterns too, so it can be used to great effect in soft furnishings and upholstery. Because the stitch covers the back of the canvas, it has hard-wearing qualities too.

STITCH COVERAGE

Always use enough strands of yarn or embroidery cotton for the gauge of your canvas. On a large gauge, such as 10-count, you will need all three strands of Paterna Persian yarn, but you can reduce this for a smaller-gauge canvas. If in doubt, try a small area of stitching on a corner of the canvas to check the cover.

It is also important not to make the stitches too long – anything over 2.5cm will need to be worked in two stitches. (See How to work long stitch overleaf). With this technique you can add textured detail to your stitching and avoid leaving long, loopy stitches.

TEXTURES AND SHADES

Using rows of abutting stitches, you can create random or geometric texturing, working each subsequent row of stitches to share the holes in which the previous row was worked. When you have completed one row of stitches, start the second row below the base of the last stitch in the first row, taking the needle back down into the bottom of the existing stitch (see steps overleaf).

Long stitch is a stabbing stitch, so you must complete one movement of the thread before bringing the needle through the canvas again. This reduces wear on the yarn or cotton and also helps to keep the canvas in shape. Make sure to keep the tension even – this is particularly important on longer stitches. The shape of the finished work will be better if you keep the canvas stretched in a frame – this will also help you keep an even tension throughout.

VERTICAL AND HORIZONTAL

Different textures can be achieved by using a mixture of vertical and horizontal stitching for different coloured areas. For details of how to abut stitching, see steps overleaf.

HOW TO WORK LONG STITCH

1 Working over the thread at the back of the canvas as you go, bring needle behind the canvas from A to come up at B, then stitch down into C, directly below B to make the next stitch.

2 BACK The reverse of a piece of long stitch shows the canvas completely covered, with the threads making a slightly diagonal pattern. This back and front coverage makes long stitch hard-wearing.

3 To avoid long stitches, break up large areas in a straight or uneven line. Complete a row of stitching; bring the thread up below the row of stitches and stitch into the shared hole immediately above.

HOW TO WORK GEOMETRIC LONG STITCH

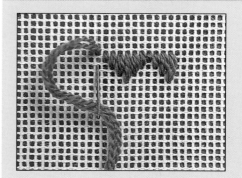

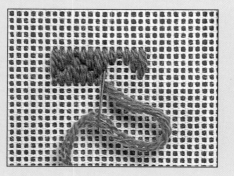

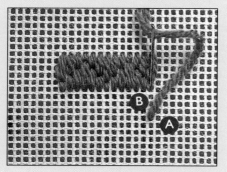

1 To make a geometric pattern, take each successive stitch on the top row one thread lower down the canvas up to five threads, then continue taking each stitch over one less thread of canvas.

2 In the next row work so the bottom of each stitch forms a line, working each stitch into a shared hole from the row before. Bring the needle up below the last stitch, mirroring a short stitch with a long one, and so on.

3 Always stab down into a hole shared with another stitch, B, and bring the needle up in an empty hole, A. This ensures that loose fibres dragged by the movement of the needle are taken under the canvas, not on the top.

DIFFERENT EFFECTS WITH COLOUR

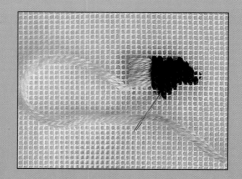

1 Use different shades of the same colour in random stitching, as in the inter-locking rows of long stitch (far left). The effect is of a smooth satin stitch with subtle variations in colour.

2 You can use long stitch horizontally and vertically together to contrast colours and textures. Be sure when stitching at a right angle to existing stitching that you finish stitches in the holes just covered by the abutting stitch.

114

Blocking canvas

*Even the most painstakingly framed and stitched needlepoint
is likely to distort slightly in the making. Here is the tried and tested
method of getting any canvas back into shape.*

The process of stitching – especially diagonal stitching, as in tent stitch and half cross-stitch – tends to pull canvas out of shape. To restore it to symmetry, you will need to stretch and 'block' the stitched work – the time this takes and the way in which you go about it will depend on how badly distorted the canvas is.

STITCHING FOR SHAPE

Keep distortion to a minimum by always having your canvas stretched in a slate frame as you work (see page 18). Also, when you stitch, keep the tension even and avoid tugging the yarn tightly – this, and using too thick a yarn, are the main causes of work taking on outlandish shapes.

The type of canvas has relatively little bearing on the way it distorts, as evenweave canvases are easier to block and stretch than interlocked ones – but the latter tend to hold their shape better anyway.

Measure up the stitching area on your canvas, or calculate the size if you are working from a chart on plain canvas, and draw an outline on a sheet of thick, preferably graph, paper. You can use this as a guide to reshape it later.

SQUARING UP

Leave a good border – at least 2 to 3cm – of canvas around the edge of your finished work, so that you have enough to get hold of when stretching and pinning it. Soften the work and make it more malleable by dampening it from the back. You can do this with a fine water spray, by wrapping it in a damp towel or by dabbing it with a wet sponge. At this stage, if the work is only slightly distorted, all you need to do is stretch it gently by hand. For very distorted canvases, you need a completely plain, unpainted, unvarnished piece of

wood larger by at least 5cm all round than the finished work and at least 1cm thick – 5-ply is ideal. You can buy blocking boards, marked in squares, especially for this purpose and this is a good investment if you do a lot of needlepoint.

Pin or tape the outline of your stitched work to the board, as in the steps overleaf. If you like, pin it over a sheet of blotting paper for absorbency. Hold the work firmly by the canvas edges and pull steadily against the distortion, then place the work on the board, pinning to the outline using drawing pins or tacks no more than 3cm apart. Keep the pins in the plain canvas so as not to pull at the

stitching and keep stretching the canvas gently into shape as you work round it. Adjust the pins more as the canvas starts to give. A badly distorted piece may need additional dampening and pinning before it can be squared up. Once you have the shape you want, leave the canvas on the board to dry in a warm, well-ventilated place, away from direct light and heat. Do not be tempted to take it off the board until it is completely dry.

Even a badly distorted canvas can be coaxed back into symmetrical shape with the help of drawing pins and a firm board.

HOW TO BLOCK A CANVAS

1 *This design, worked in continental tent stitch, should be square but it has been pulled out of shape by the diagonal slant of the stitching. The distortion might have been less had the work been kept taut in a frame.*

2 *Draw an outline of the work as it should be on graph paper and mark the centre of each side, using a pencil or waterproof pen. Pin the graph paper to a 5-ply or other type of thick wooden board.*

3 *Dampen the stitched canvas thoroughly by sponging it from the back with warm water (as above) or by using a fine spray on the back, or rolling the canvas in a wet white or colourfast towel.*

4 *Grip the damp canvas firmly by the unstitched edges and pull steadily against the distortion to get the canvas into a better shape before you start to block it on the prepared wooden board.*

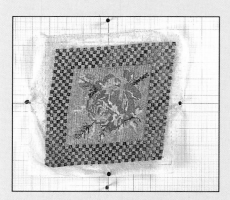

5 *Pin the canvas over the outline on the board, matching the centre of each side to the marked points. Pin the corners out to match the shape with pins 3cm apart.*

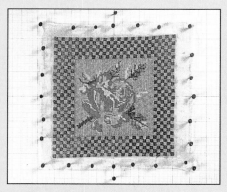

6 *Use a set square or the corner of a magazine to check that each corner is a right angle. Restretch if necessary. Allow the canvas to dry completely before removing it.*

MILD DISTORTION

If your canvas is only slightly distorted, you might not need to go through the full stretching and blocking process. Often all you need to do is press the canvas from the back using a steam iron, then pull the canvas firmly back into shape by hand. If this is not enough, dampen the canvas further by placing a damp towel between the iron and the canvas, then pin the work out as in the steps on the left. Always make sure the stitching has dried completely before you unpin it from the board or it may start to contract.

BLOCKING MACHINE

An investment for very keen needle-point stitchers, the blocking machine shown above does all the work for you. As they are relatively expensive to buy, they are certainly not worth the cost for the occasional stitcher – you may like to use instead the blocking service offered by some wool companies as advertised in magazines.

Mitring corners

Carefully mitred corners add a professional-looking finish to embroidered items. Try these easy methods for perfect results every time.

There are several ways of finishing off the corners of an embroidered project neatly, but one of the most attractive and least conspicuous methods is by mitring the corners. Mitring involves stitching angled seams in the turning allowed for the hem. These seams are worked at a 45° angle to the corner edges of the finished item, and give a very neat finish.

USES FOR MITRED CORNERS

Depending on your exact method of finishing, mitres can be worked so that they appear on the wrong side or the right side of the work. Mitres on the wrong side will obviously not show so much, and are excellent for pieces of decorative household linen, such as tray cloths, table mats and tablecloths, when you want a neat and hard-wearing hem with precise corners. One of the main benefits of mitring is that it reduces the bulk at the corners of the embroidered item, so the corners are flatter than if you finish them by simply folding them over square.

For other types of embroidery you may prefer to work the mitres so that they appear on the right side of your work. This method is useful if you want to catch down a hem with a decorative stitch such as herringbone, so that it becomes a feature of the design. You can also cover the raw fabric edges with a decorative strip, such as bias binding, lace or *broderie anglaise*. This technique works particularly well if you are working with a bulky fabric or a loosely woven one that frays or distorts easily, as you only have to turn over one thickness of the fabric for the hem.

MITRING METHODS

Although mitring gives professional-looking results, it is very easy to achieve; there is no mystique to it, just careful technique. The most important thing to watch is the first pressing under of the diagonal fold; you must be very careful not to pull or stretch the fabric at this stage; if it is distorted, the mitre will not lie quite flat. Evenweave fabrics are sometimes very loosely woven and easily distorted; you may find it useful to give the flat corners a quick press with spray-on starch before you begin the folding. This will give the corners a temporary stability while you work on them and also help to prevent the edges from fraying at the same time.

You also need to make sure that the fold is at exactly 45° to the edges of the stitched item. On evenweave fabrics this is easy to do as you can line up the raw edges of the folded corner with the warp and weft threads of the fabric. With other fabrics, you may find it useful just to hold the fold against a protractor before you press it, to make sure that the angle is accurate. Once all the corners of the embroidery have been mitred, the hem can be stitched as usual.

The photographs below show the back and the front view of a neatly mitred corner.

HOW TO MITRE A CORNER ON THE BACK

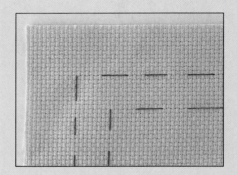

1 Tack along the fold line around the edges of your work, then tack another line the depth of your desired hem inside the first line. Trim your fabric to the depth of your hem plus 8mm for turnings.

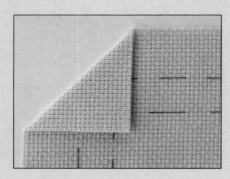

2 Fold the corner of the fabric to the wrong side at an angle of exactly 45° so that the fold just touches the corner of the outer line of tacking. Press firmly with a steam iron to give a crisp line.

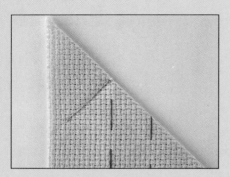

3 Unfold the corner, then fold the fabric in half diagonally, right sides together, so the two parts of the pressed line match. Stitch by hand or machine along the pressed line, from the fold to within 8mm of the raw edges.

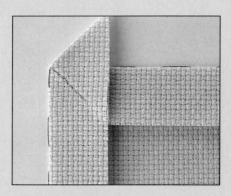

4 Open out the mitre corner and press the fabric firmly along the outer tacked line, so that the hem lies flat on the right side of the fabric.

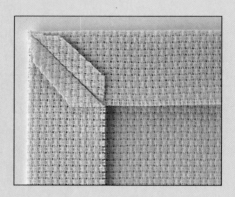

5 Trim the mitred seam and clip the corners to remove the excess fabric. Press the seam open so that it lies flat. Remove the outer line of tacking stitches.

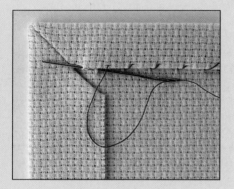

6 Turn the hem to the wrong side and press. Turn under the extra allowance so that the hem lies folded along the second tacked line. Press, remove tacking, and stitch down hem.

HOW TO MITRE A CORNER ON THE FRONT

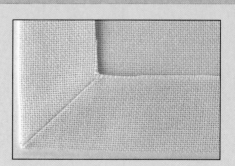

The easiest method is to stitch the mitre in the usual way, but work with the wrong sides of the work together and stitch the seam right out to the raw edges of the folded line.

For a decorative effect, stitch a strip of binding or ribbon to cover the raw edges. Mitre the binding or ribbon by stitching diagonal seams on the wrong sides at the corners.

WHAT WENT WRONG?

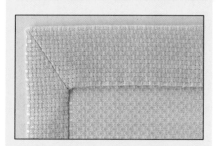

Here, the original fold for the mitre was not made at exactly 45°. As a result. the mitre is crooked; although it lies neatly, the unequal angles make the hem allowances uneven.

Making cushion pads

One of the secrets of successful cushion-making is having the right cushion pad. Here we show how to make your own.

I f you want a pad for an unusual shape or size of cushion or just want to economise, it is useful to know how to make your own. Making cushion pads is straightforward; the steps are logical and can easily be adapted for different shapes and sizes.

FABRICS FOR CUSHION PADS

The best fabrics to use are firmly woven cottons. These are easy to work with, keep their shape well without distorting under the pressure of the stuffing, and are cheap and readily available. It is best to choose white or cream, in case your cushion cover is thin and the pad shows through, though if you are making pads especially for dark cushion covers you can use up left-overs of dark cotton fabric.

Firmly woven cambric, cotton sheeting or similar fabrics are very good and usually cheap. Chintzes and polished cottons can be used and are more expensive. Many people use calico, which is cheap. The dressing that is used on some cotton fabrics, including calico, as well as the firm weave help the fabric – and therefore the cushion pad – to keep its shape. If you are using feathers or down as a stuffing, it is worth paying more for down-proof cotton. If you don't, the feathers will work their way through the fabric.

STUFFINGS FOR CUSHION PADS

Many materials are available as filling for cushion pads. Your choice will probably depend on the size and type of the cushion, the desired texture of the finished cushion and how much money you want to spend.

The most expensive stuffing is **feathers**, or a mixture of feathers and down. Down is the extra-fluffy feather-like material that grows under a bird's main feathers. Feathers and down give a smooth, satisfactory finish with just the right amount of squash or give.

Foam chips are cheap and readily available. They give a springy feel and can be quite hard if the cushion is firmly stuffed. The smaller the chips, the better, but avoid cheap chips full of big, firm lumps, and make sure that any foam you use is flame-retardant.

Polystyrene balls are ideal for large floor cushions or items for which you need a filling that moves to take on the required shape. These too are very cheap, but they can give off noxious fumes if they catch fire. Also they do eventually compress, so you will have to top up the cushion filling after a while.

Other stuffings include **kapok**, a natural stuffing which is soft but which can tend to flatten or become lumpy, and **polyester filling**, which is washable.

When making your own cushion pads, bear in mind the safety aspect of the materials you plan to use. Whenever possible, choose flame-retardant fabrics and fillings. Also bear in mind that most needlepoint cushions will not be easily washable and choose a stuffing that can by dry-cleaned if possible.

Feather

Down

Foam chips

Polystyrene balls

Kapok

Polyester filling

HOW TO MAKE A SQUARE CUSHION PAD

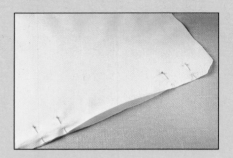

1 Cut two squares of fabric the size you want your finished cushion pad to be plus seam allowances. Machine round the seam line, leaving several inches open in one side.

2 Clip the corners, turn right side out and press. Fill with the stuffing through the gap; don't over-stuff, otherwise the cushion will be too firm.

3 Fold under the raw edges around the gap; pin them together, then stitch neatly close to the outside of the fabric to close the opening.

HOW TO MAKE A CIRCULAR CUSHION PAD WITH A GUSSET

1 Cut two circles the size of your pad plus seam allowances. Measure the circumference. Cut a gusset to this length by the required depth, plus seam allowances.

2 To make the gusset, seam the ends of the fabric strip to form a circle, then pin, tack and stitch around one circle, right sides together, easing the fabric round the curve.

3 Attach the gusset to the other circle in the same way, leaving a gap for stuffing. Trim the seams, then turn, stuff and close by hand- or machine stitching.

bright idea

For a scented or herbal cushion, put some pot pourri or fragrant dried herbs inside the cushion pad. Mix them with some stuffing as well, otherwise the cushion will be too hard and lumpy.

WHAT WENT WRONG?

It is important to get just the right amount of stuffing in your pad. The aqua cushion has been filled with a pad that is too big and too firmly stuffed; the shape is distorted, and the cushion has no squash or give. The checked cushion has a pad that is too small and flat; it has lost all its shape, and cannot provide any support.

Applying piping

Piping in a matching or contrasting fabric sets off all manner of cushions and upholstery to perfection. Here's how to achieve a professional finish.

To show an embroidered, or indeed any, type of cushion off to look its very best, trim it with piping in a colour and fabric of your choice. It is not at all difficult and gives a neat, professional edge. A variety of effects can be achieved by using piping in a complementary colour to the cushion, in a contrasting colour, or of a different texture.

MAKING PIPING

Although it is possible to buy ready-made piping in standard colours, or braid specially set on a strip which can be applied like piping, making your own is very easy.

When you are buying piping cord, you will first need to measure the edges of the cushion which you wish to trim and allow at least 10cm for turning and fraying. If you intend to wash the finished cushion cover, it is a good idea to wash the piping cord itself before you apply it in case it shrinks.

Select a gauge of cord which will suit the weight of the fabric and size of the cushion. Now you can choose whether you want to use ready-made bias binding or cut bias strips in a fabric to match your cushion.

For bias binding simply buy the same length as the piping cord, in a width that will leave you at least 1.5cm seam allowance when it is doubled over the cord. Bias-cut fabric stretches around corners so it is ideal for this kind of trimming for cushions, but if you want to make your own binding from a piece of material, you will need to cut bias strips of fabric.

CUTTING BINDING

First lay out your fabric as shown in the steps overleaf and fold the horizontal grain of one end up to lie along the vertical grain. Press the fabric along this fold with a warm iron and then cut along the fold. Now all you need to do is cut strips of the required width, keeping them parallel to the first cut. Cut a width which will leave 1.5cm of doubled fabric free when folded over the cord.

To trim a whole cushion, you will need to join several strips – do this following step 3 to make a continuous strip. Press the turned seam so it lies flat and trim the edges evenly.

To make the piping itself, fold the binding in half along its length, wrong sides together, to enclose the cord. Pin and tack firmly so that the stitching is right next to the piping cord.

APPLYING THE PIPING

Lay out the fabric for the cushion front, right side up, and mark a 1.5cm seam allowance all round. Take the piping and, starting in the centre of one side, pin the piping along the seam line, the cord lying just inside the seamline, carefully shaping it around the corners.

When you come to join the two ends of piping in the seam, cut the cord inside the two pieces to abut exactly and cut the binding on one end level with the cord. Trim the binding on the other end to within 3cm of the end of the piping and fold under a 1.5cm turning. Pull this end over the other end of piping to cover it like a sleeve. Then, making sure it is lying flat, pin and tack in place all round.

Stitch the piping in place, either by hand in backstitch, or by machine using a zipper or piping foot to keep the stitching close to the piping cord. Snip the corners of the binding inside the seam so they lie flat at the corners. Place the cushion back over the front, right sides together. Pin and tack in place around three sides and stitch over the previous line of stitching.

Fill the cushion with a suitable pad, then fold back a 1.5cm turning down the edge of the backing, and fold in the piped edge along the line of the stitching. Pin the two together and tack in place, then slip stitch together to complete the cushion.

Choose a fabric to complement the cushion colour for a really professional finish.

HOW TO MAKE PIPING

1 *Mark the horizontal straight grain of the piping fabric and fold it up to meet the vertical grain. Press this diagonal fold to form a sharp crease, then cut along the fold to give one edge of the bias binding.*

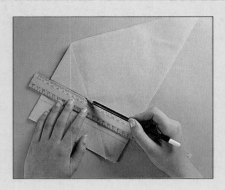

2 *Depending on the thickness of your piping cord, mark lines an appropriate width from the diagonal you have cut, keeping them parallel. Cut strips to give the length of binding you need.*

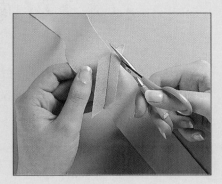

3 *To join two strips of binding, place two ends right sides together so that they form a right-angle. Make a 1.5cm seam, then press open so that the binding forms a continuous strip. Snip off the triangle edges.*

4 *Take the piping cord (washed if necessary to prevent shrinkage) and lay along the centre of the wrong side of the binding. Fold to enclose piping cord, matching the edges, and pin and tack next to the cord.*

5 *Press the fabric for the cushion front and mark a 1.5cm seam line all round it. Pin the piping to the right side of the fabric, matching the tacked line to the seam line and curving the piping at the corners.*

6 *Where piping ends meet, cut the cord to abut and trim one end of binding level with its cord. Leave 3cm overlap of binding on the other end, turn under 1.5cm and cover the short end. Pin in place.*

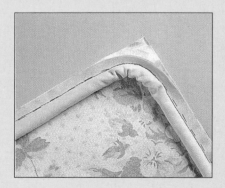

7 *Stitch the piping to the cushion front either by hand using backstitch or by machine using a piping foot to keep the stitching close to the piping cord all the way round.*

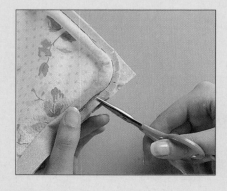

8 *At the corners, snip the binding to within a couple of threads from stitching so that it fans out and lies evenly against the cushion front. Press and mark a seam allowance on the cushion back.*

9 *Attach cushion back to the front on three sides, right sides together, pinning along the stitching and keeping the cord inside the seam. Turn right side out, insert pad; turn in open edges and slip stitch.*

Cords, braids & tassels

Making your own cords and braids is surprisingly easy, and they can be used to add the perfect finishing touch to all kinds of projects, from cushion covers to accessories and garments.

Cords and braids have many uses to the needleworker. You can make fine or textured versions and incorporate them into needlepoint and embroidery projects, or use thicker cords for couching down with stitches in a contrasting thread. Or you may find that you want an edging for a piece of embroidery, such as a cushion cover. For all these different uses, it is very satisfying to make just the kind of cord or braid you want, in exactly the right thickness, using the perfect colours of thread.

WHAT ARE CORDS AND BRAIDS?

Cords are simply twisted hanks of thread. The mistake that many people make when they are making their own cords is to use only a single twist of threads. Stable cords, which do not unravel easily, are formed from double twists, where the batch of threads has been twisted tightly and then allowed to double back on itself. It is much easier to use a cord for your projects when it is not trying to unravel itself all the time.

Braids are plaits of threads. The traditional braid is made from three hanks of threads plaited together, and this is the easiest

kind to make if you are a beginner, but if you are good at plaiting you will know that more than three hanks can be plaited at the same time. The principle is the same, but using more hanks takes a little practice, and is best done on a flat surface such as a macramé board so that you can see where you are. If you use hanks of different colours, you will be able to see very easily whether you have kept the hanks in the right order as you plait.

MATERIALS TO USE

Both cords and braids can be made using the same thread throughout, or using a mixture of many different threads. You can make both cords and braids with any kind of thread, from the finest silk to the thickest yarn, but remember that some threads are so fine that you will need many lengths to make a braid or cord of a significant thickness.

If you want a very fine cord or braid, you will need to use a very fine thread to make it, or use just a few strands of a coarser thread. So, for instance, for a fine cord to edge a silk-

covered box, you could twist quite a large number of strands of silk thread, which is very delicate and twists very tightly, or just a few strands of a thicker thread such as pearl cotton. If you want a thick cord, you could use many strands of fine thread such as stranded cotton, or just a few strands of a thick wool. Remember, though, that if you are making a cord, the final cord will be twice the thickness that you see when you have made the preliminary twist, because you allow it to double back on itself.

Both cords and braids look very effective made in a selection of threads of different colours and textures. If you are making an edging for a particular project, try to use the left-over threads from the project itself, blending the colours so that they reflect the colour mix in the piece of work. If you are making something for a subtle piece of work, blend the colours of your cord or braid subtly; similarly, if you are making an edging for a bright, bold piece, be more adventurous with your colour choice for your cords and braids.

The cords and braids shown here can be home-made, using threads varying from thick, soft cottons to fine metallics. These examples demonstrate well the different effects you can achieve by varying the colours, textures and thicknesses of threads.

HOW TO MAKE A FINGER BRAID

1 Wind a hank of thread twice the required length of the braid. Cut the looped edges at the bottom. Secure the top to a solid object, such as a chair back, or with a drawing pin.

2 Divide the large hank into three equal hanks of thread and begin plaiting them, taking the hank from each side in turn and weaving it over and under the others.

3 When you have plaited the whole length of the threads, secure the end with a knot so that the braid cannot unravel. The braid is now ready for you to use.

HOW TO MAKE A FINGER CORD

1 Cut lengths of thread three times the required length of the cord. Knot the ends. Tie or hook the top around something solid, or pin it securely to a wooden surface.

2 Using a pencil, keep the hank taut and twist the threads steadily in one direction until you have twisted the whole hank firmly. Bring the end of the hank up to the top.

3 If you have made the preliminary twist firm enough but not too tight, the two halves of the cord will twist smoothly and securely together and will not unravel.

bright ideas

There are endless threads and yarns that can be used to create unusual cords and braids. In these two examples, knitting yarns have been used to create textured effects.

The upper example is a plaited finger braid which has been made from three fancy knitting yarns of the same weight.

In the lower example, a mohair knitting yarn and a smooth ribbon yarn have been combined to make a twisted finger cord. This has been loosely wound to make the most of the sheen on the ribbon yarn.

WHAT WENT WRONG?

Your cord will not work properly if it is twisted too tightly. In the example shown here, the cord has been over-wound so that it has become distorted and irregular instead of forming a neat, double twist.

HALF CROSS-STITCH

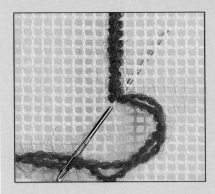

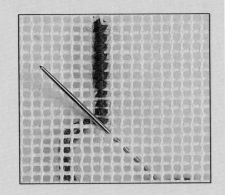

For a vertical row of stitches, bring the needle out and make the stitch in the hole diagonally below and left. Start the next stitch in the hole to the right of the thread.

A vertical row of half cross-stitch produces horizontal stitches on the back. Conversely, a horizontal row gives vertical stitches on the reverse of the work.

LACING A PICTURE

One way of mounting needlepoint over a piece of stiff card for a picture is to lace it across the back. Use strong buttonhole thread and begin lacing from the centre of one long side out towards the edge, securing the thread firmly. Pass the thread across from one side to the other in zigzag steps, taking a small stitch several canvas threads in from the edge at regular intervals. Pull the canvas taut as you go. Fasten the buttonhole thread off securely.

Complete lacing the long side by working out from the centre again to the other edge. Fold the corners under neatly on the short sides and then lace these together from top to bottom in the same way as for the long sides.

ALPHABET

Make up your messages using the letters and numbers on the chart above stitched in Holbein stitch.

Mail-order kits

As an added benefit to our readers, we are able to offer a selection of the projects in this book as mail-order kits. All the cross-stitch kits include aida fabric, needle, Madeira 6-stranded embroidery cottons, stitch chart and instructions; all the needlepoint projects include plain canvas, needle, Paterna Persian pure wool tapestry yarn, stitch chart and instructions.

ORDERING BY POST

Simply photocopy or cut out the order form opposite, fill it in and post it.

Please check that your name, address and postcode are correct and that your cheque or credit card instructions are completed and signed.

UK ORDERS

Post your order to the Readicut address below with payment either by cheque/postal order or by Visa/Mastercard/Switchcard.

For orders under £25.00, add £1.95 for postage, packing and insurance; for orders over £25.00, add £2.95.

Cheques and postal orders should be made payable to **Readicut Wool** and crossed **/and Co./**.

EUROPEAN ORDERS

Post your completed order form to the UK Readicut address below left with payment only by Visa/Mastercard.

For orders under £25.00, add £4.95 for postage, packing and insurance; for orders over £25.00, add £6.95. Delivery will be by air mail. (Customers are liable for any local duty payable.)

AUSTRALIAN AND NEW ZEALAND ORDERS

For prices and availability, please contact:

Needlecraft Mailbox
PO Box 816
Gosford
NSW 2250
AUSTRALIA
Tel. (043) 231155

REST OF THE WORLD

Post your completed order form to the UK Readicut address below left with payment only by Visa/Mastercard.

For all orders, add £10.95 for postage, packing and insurance. Delivery will be by surface mail. (Customers are liable for any local duty payable.)

ORDERING BY PHONE

Phone our 24-hour telephone ordering line to place your order:

Tel. 01924 810810
(Int. +44 1924 810810)

The Craft Collection Ltd
Registered Office:
Terry Mills, Horbury, West Yorkshire
Registered Number: 271932 England

READICUT WOOL
TERRY MILLS
OSSETT
WEST YORKSHIRE
WF5 9SA

Should you not require any of the offers listed opposite, you may still like a **FREE** copy of Readicut's 76-page catalogue *READICUT CRAFTS,* which is packed with a superb range of needlecraft kits, canvases, fabrics, Paterna Persian pure wool tapestry yarn, Madeira 6-stranded embroidery cotton, accessories and much more. Send your name and address to Readicut (address on left) and Readicut will rush a copy to you by return.

Order Form

ITEM	CODE	DESCRIPTION	QTY	PRICE	£ : p
1	72438	**Garden flower cushion kit** (page 13)		£17.99	:
2	72498	**Baroque cushion kit** (page 21)		£17.99	:
3	72562	**Victorian sampler kit** (page 25)		£10.99	:
4	78330	**First home sampler kit** (page 43)		£10.99	:
5	72576	**Aesop's fables pictures kit** (page 67)		£10.99	:
6	78332	**Gold frame kit** (page 75)		£9.99	:
7	78340	**Cornucopia picture kit** (page 83)		£9.99	:

TOTAL VALUE OF GOODS	:
ADD P&P AND INSURANCE* *UK:* £1.95 for orders under £25.00, £2.95 for orders over £25.00. *Europe:* £4.95 for orders under £25.00, £6.95 for orders over £25.00. *Rest of World:* £10.95 for all orders.	:
TOTAL ORDER VALUE	:

If you do not wish to receive direct mail from other companies please tick ☐

TITLE................INITIALS ....

SURNAME..

ADDRESS...

....

....

POSTCODE ....

Delivery – your order will normally be despatched within 48 hours of receipt. At our busy times this may take a little longer, but we promise to get your order to you as quickly as possible.

Guarantee – all our products are covered by our money-back guarantee. In the unlikely event of your not being entirely satisfied with your order, return the item in a clean, resaleable condition within 14 days of receipt and your money will be refunded.

All offers are subject to availability

OFFICE USE ONLY

PAYMENT METHOD (Please tick appropriate box)

CHEQUE/PO ☐   Value enclosed:

CREDIT CARD ☐   £

Charge my Visa/Mastercard/Switchcard* No.

☐☐☐☐ ☐☐☐☐ ☐☐☐☐ ☐☐☐☐ ☐☐

Signature ....

EXPIRY DATE ....*SWITCH ISSUE / VERSION NO. ☐☐

Should your order form be completed incorrectly we reserve the right to charge to your account the correct amount due for the goods described on your order.

Index